Yale Romanic Studies, Second Series, 17

Music and the *Musician in*
JEAN-CHRISTOPHE:

The Harmony of Contrasts

by David Sices

New Haven and London, Yale University Press, 1968

15 17 15

To my late father, Harry Sices,
in gratitude.

Acknowledgments

My heartfelt thanks go to Professors Henri Peyre and Victor Brombert, of Yale University; Eugene H. Falk, of the University of North Carolina; and Lawrence E. Harvey, of Dartmouth College, for their encouragement, aid and criticism in the writing of this study;

to Madame Marie Romain-Rolland, for her cordial welcome and patient help in my consultation of the Fonds Romain Rolland in Paris;

to the trustees and officers of Dartmouth College, for the three-month research leave which made possible the extensive revisions of my original manuscript.

The last chapter of this book originally appeared, in slightly different form, as an article in *The French Review*. My thanks go to Professor John W. Kneller, Editor, for his kind permission to use it here.

D.S.

Table of Contents

I. INTRODUCTION

Romain Rolland and Music

> Il est clair que je n'ai jamais prétendu écrire un roman . . . .
> Qu'est-ce donc que cette oeuvre? . . . C'est un homme que j'ai
> créé. La vie d'un homme ne s'enferme point dans le cadre d'une
> forme littéraire. Sa loi est en elle; et chaque vie a sa loi . . . .
> Certaines vies humaines sont des lacs tranquilles, d'autres de
> grands cieux clairs où voguent les nuages, d'autres des plaines
> fécondes, d'autres des cimes déchiquetées. *Jean-Christophe* m'est
> apparu comme un fleuve.[1]

These lines, written by Romain Rolland in 1909 as a preface to
Dans la Maison, contain the elements of *Jean-Christophe*'s "grandeur
et misère" in the eyes of contemporary criticism. They epitomize
Rolland's disdain for his craft and for the tradition of the literary
genre; his tendency to think in high-sounding, idealistic, but often
vague analogies, which confuse hero and work, life and art; and
his exclusive concentration, from a literary point of view, on the
larger-than-life subjectivity, the monstrously distended ego of his
musician-hero. It is understandable that a critic like Henri Peyre,
oriented toward the classical virtues and economy of the traditional
French "roman d'analyse," would classify *Jean-Christophe* as symptomatic of a period he calls "a low point in the history of French
fiction." [2]

Romain Rolland himself seems, in his "Adieu à Jean Christophe"
(p. 1595), deeply thankful at having finally succeeded in killing off
his hero: "Moi-même, je dis adieu à mon âme passée; je la rejette
derrière moi, comme une enveloppe vide." He permitted himself
even clearer expressions of weariness after the eight years of public

---

1. "Aux amis de Jean-Christophe," *Jean-Christophe,* Édition Définitive (1 vol.
Paris, Albin Michel, 1961), p. 1600.
2. Henri Peyre, *The Contemporary French Novel,* p. 24.

life—and ten previous years of private meditation—which carried his hero from birth to final rest. Rolland's published corespondence with Jean-Richard Bloch and Sofia Bertolini, two of his intimate confidants, contains eloquent expression of his sense of relief at the conclusion of the roman-fleuve which had gained him an enduring reputation but usurped his attention and energies for too long.

Yet it is precisely this untraditional (to some, "un-French") distortion of the normal proportions of the novel and character that seems to have attracted its vast and passionate public. It is still principally *Jean-Christophe* which accounts today for Rolland's reputation, for the thirteen doctoral dissertations on him in progress at the Sorbonne, for example, attested to by Jacques Robichez in 1961.[3] The novel's partisans have found from the beginning a sense of reassuring grandeur in this German musician's struggles, passions, and victories, which derives immediately from its peculiarly nonliterary techniques and structure. Few literary works of its period can claim to have evoked so violent and so profound a reaction from their appreciators and detractors and to have exerted such a deep moral influence on their time.

To understand why a work of "anti-literature" has had this popular acclaim and has even been granted high intellectual importance in spite of its artistic flaws, *Jean-Christophe* must be examined in the light of the other great art it is meant to promote and to embody: music. The place Rolland's musician-hero was to have in the lives and hearts of his public is inextricably connected with the reasons which led at least one encyclopedia of music to call it "the world's greatest musical novel." *Jean-Christophe* is incomprehensible today without reference to the moral revolution connected with the revival of musical interest in France during the first two decades of this century. This phenomenon in turn can most strikingly be illustrated and explained by the important and varied roles which Romain Rolland played, as musicologist, historian, journalist, critic, teacher, biographer, and novelist, during the twenty-five years of his public career preceding the First World War.

We intend to study Rolland's place and importance in the musical life of this period, the tendencies and influences which contributed

3. *Romain Rolland*, p. 235.

to the development of his peculiar conception of the nature and function of music, and the ways in which this conception enters into character, technique, and structure in *Jean-Christophe*. If it is beyond the scope and the competency of this study to redefine the place of Rolland's novel in the history of twentieth-century French fiction, it can still be hoped that a more just estimate of its strengths and flaws, its grandeur and its weakness, will emerge.

In a sense, Rolland's most enduring creation, his most impressive monument, is his life itself. His appreciators have always admired his intransigent adherence to what he felt to be justice and truth, his dedication to unpopular causes in spite of frequently violent censure, as well as his patient interest in the trials and sufferings of correspondents and petitioners. It is apparent that this admiration has affected the literary judgment of his contemporaries and their successors, who are prone to see the excellent qualities of Rolland the man in his novel and its hero. Without losing sight of the critic's obligation to understand and judge a literary work on its own merits, no matter how interesting or admirable its author, the first part of this study will pay special attention to those elements of Rolland's intellectual, emotional, and professional experience which contributed to the formulation of his idea of music and the musician, their nature and function, and its transformation in the literary form of *Jean-Christophe*. Chief among these will be the succession of philosophic revelations or "éclairs" which he underwent before and during his stay at the "cloître de la rue d'Ulm" (the Ecole Normale Supérieure): the influence of Spinoza, Renan, and Tolstoy; his orientation toward an academic career in the field of cultural history and musicology; the gradual development of his commitment to humanitarian principles in the fields of art and politics and their conflict with more internal currents of his creative ideal; and the series of events—the honors, failures, positions, friendships, and contacts with "history"—which most influenced the shape and character of Rolland's chief literary work.

The Credo quia verum

The circumstances surrounding Romain Rolland's choice of a field of specialization at the Ecole Normale shed useful light on his later ideas concerning music history. His diary of the period, published as *Le Cloître de la rue d'Ulm,*[4] is a logbook of sentiments, intuitions, maxims, and philosophic meditations hinting at his future intellectual development. Many of these are directly connected with the professional direction he was beginning to take at that time; others reveal the psychological and experiential factors which led Rolland into the field of history.

It is evident from Rolland's notes that necessity and personal interest were among the factors influencing his decision. The possibility of missions and voyages abroad and the relatively quick academic promotion in the field seem to have appealed to Rolland's ambition and promised fulfillment of old desires. In addition, personal antipathy and intellectual incompatibility turned him away from the professors of philosophy, Ollé-Laprune and Brochard, while Paul Guiraud and Gabriel Monod, in history, had been from the beginning among the most attractive of his professors. There was no question, seemingly, of studying literature under Brunetière, for whom Rolland nurtured an abiding distaste. The groundwork for Rolland's lasting estrangement from the French literary "establishment" was already being laid at this early date. But along with numerous artistic and intellectual discoveries which fill the notes of this period, there is a recurrent, almost obsessive attempt to arrive at philosophical bases for life and action. These passages cast a most revealing illumination on Rolland's deeper reasons for undertaking a career in the study of history, and specifically the history of music.

Out of Rolland's reaction to the idealist bias of his philosophy classes, his experience of the "éclairs," and his discussions with classmates, especially André Suarès, developed a philosophical credo which he formulated during his second year at the Ecole Normale under the title *Credo quia verum,* in contradiction to the pseudo-Augustinian *Credo quia absurdum.* If this spiritual testament bears eloquent witness to the youth of its writer in its passionate search for identity and "reality," in its axioms and abstractions, it also displays an impressive accordance with the direction Rolland's life and thought were to take years later. Many elements of it can be

4. In *Cahiers Romain Rolland, 4.*

found in *Jean-Christophe,* as stages in the composer's spiritual development or as part of his final character.

Rolland's chief concern was to reconcile his individual ego with the outside world and with universal being. Rejecting Cartesian rationalism, he starts from a parody formula, as in his title: "Je sens, donc Il Est." From the primary evidence of sensation, he derives proof not so much of his own existence as an individual, but of "Its" existence, the existence of something of which he is part, which is infinite and eternal. Out of sensation comes knowledge of both individual and universal being.

Two aspects of this axiom are especially relevant to Rolland's ideas on musical history: the basic cognitive role of the intuition as opposed to reason; and the sense of expanding and overflowing life which links not only the individual manifestations of universal being in space, but the durational sequence of these individuals and groups across time. Rolland is preoccupied, even at this early date, with death, the spatial and temporal continuity of human life, and the problem of the individual soul's relation with the collective soul and its other individuations. The credo is addressed "to suffering spirits": already Rolland was spiritually divided between the powerful current of egotistical force he felt in himself and the call of his fellowmen. His answer to this conflict is that the ego far exceeds its individual envelope or "rôle," that it exists in all and for all time.

> *Je* suis Romain Rolland, et en chacune de ses sensations. Mais *Je* le déborde, *Je* suis en dehors de lui. *Je* suis tous ceux qui l'entourent, l'univers des âmes et des corps. Sous les formes innombrables, sans cesse, *J'*évolue, dans Mon Présent immense et mouvant.[5]

In terms of Rolland's plan for living, the ideal would consist therefore of reconciling "la sérénité souriante, la paix ironique: Platon, Goethe, Renan"; "l'ardeur de la passion (Renaissance Italienne)"; and "la charité de Tolstoy"—a challenging task for a twenty-two-year-old budding historian. The implications for Rolland's career are

---

5. *Cloître,* p. 362.

evident, however. The study of history was for him a way of exploiting his sense of penetration, his intuition of the continuity of the human soul. Rolland's preference was for those places and periods which were most strongly characterized by passion and the acts of passion. From his penetration of the events and psychological movement of human history, he hoped to bring knowledge, comfort, and aid to action, to his fellowmen. For the moment, he seems not to have realized fully the privileged role that music might play in that "histoire des âmes" which Guiraud had shrewdly seen him writing. The young scholar was irresistibly drawn to the Renaissance, because of its spectacle of action, struggle, and passion, of overflowing life.

From the first, Rolland, like Suarès, was attracted to the France, Italy, and Germany of the sixteenth century. He considered for a while specializing in the latter country—which is not surprising in view of the later consideration he was to give to German music, culminating in *Jean-Christophe*. In 1888, however, he writes: "Un de mes projets,—si je vis, est d'écrire une histoire, d'une espèce toute nouvelle. Comme époque, je choisirais la seconde moitié du XVIe siècle, les guerres de religion et de la Ligue." [6] His reasons for choosing this period are implicit in a "new kind" of historical writing, "l'histoire des âmes." First, for him the wars of religion, like the Italian Renaissance, were characterized by "a throng of powerful, complex, active individualities," requiring a historical approach based on the individual personality, on penetration of the individual soul and its action on those about it. Second, this penetration of forceful individualities demanded of the historian an ability to enter into each of them in turn, to achieve an intuitional union with his passions, sentiments, crimes, loves—a sort of momentary marriage with his personality. Third, this union with the historical character partook of that universal love of individuations of the Whole, which Rolland prescribed for himself in the third precept of his *Credo quia verum*: the charity of Tolstoy. In choosing these great figures of a great age, Rolland found it easy to experience the charity demanded of him by this ethic:

6. Ibid., p. 175.

Tous les grands acteurs de luttes sanglantes, généralement haïs ou méprisés, ont dans l'âme des parties excellentes; tous ils aiment quelqu'un ou quelque chose; et c'est pour cela qu'il faut les aimer . . . . Un seul moyen de bien comprendre et de bien peindre les personnages historiques: c'est de les aimer.[7]

This historical approach, then, was to be a history of superior souls, viewed from within, intuitively, in accordance with Rolland's first metaphysical approach to knowledge. It was a reaction against realism, or rather, in Rolland's eyes, a more valid realism, unobscured by the scientific and objective limitations of naturalism. "L'histoire réaliste n'est pas écrite," he wrote. The only certain approach to the understanding of the nature of other individuals lay in comprehending them as we do ourselves. Otherwise the historian risks seeing only the roles which the objects of his study play, not the essence of their characters and the motivation of their actions in all its complexity. Naturalistic history limits itself a priori to a partial truth: strictly observable phenomena. In so doing, it is unable to penetrate the spirit of a historical period, the peculiar moral and spiritual atmosphere which prevails at a given time and which, according to Rolland, should be the primary object of historical investigation.

During the two years Rolland spent in Rome, following his studies at the Ecole Normale, he had the opportunity to develop the way in which this sort of historiography could be incorporated into literary projects. His journals of this period reflect the genesis of a series of historical dramas which occupied the first phase of his creative writing. From *Orsino* and *Les Baglioni,* the first of his Renaissance plays (1890 and 1891), the series was to stretch through his *Tragédies de la Foi* (1893-95) to the *Théâtre de la Révolution* (1898-1902).

At the same time, Rolland's musical inclinations were beginning to penetrate his literary and historical projects. As early as August 1890, he wrote to Malwida von Meysenbug of a planned "musical novel or poem," which he described as "un peu le roman de Beethoven." Here again, it is a question of entering intuitively into the spirit of the man and his times in order to bring them to life.

7. Ibid.

Before discussing the place of Rolland in the musicology of his time, it would be useful to indicate the chronology of his professorial career, leading up to the time of his greatest influence. From the moment of his return from Italy, via Bayreuth, he became more and more involved in the world of the Sorbonne, from which he was eventually to seek escape. Having completed in Rome his *mémoire d'étude,* concisely entitled *L'histoire des négociations diplomatiques depuis le sac de Rome jusqu'à la paix de Cambrai, d'après les lettres et instructions du Cardinal Salviati, légat en France de juin 1527 à août 1529, et les documents du temps,* he turned, in Paris, toward a study of the music of the sixteenth and seventeenth centuries, which was to result in his doctoral thesis: *Les Origines du théâtre lyrique moderne. L'Histoire de l'Opéra en Europe avant Lully et Scarlatti.* Rolland's parallel interest in painting is manifested by his *thèse supplémentaire: Cur ars picturae apud italos XVI° Saeculi deciderit* (published in French as *De la Décadence de la peinture italienne au XVIe siècle*).[8] Both received very honorable mention when they were presented to the Sorbonne in 1895, and his main thesis received the Prix Kastner-Bourgault from the Academy in 1896.

Romain Rolland and Musicology

It seems surprising that Rolland's doctoral thesis was only the second of a musical nature to be presented to the University. Indeed, it was the first in the field of music history, its predecessor having been an aesthetic study defended the previous year by his future colleague and journalistic collaborator, Jules Combarieu: *Les Rapports de la musique et de la poésie considérés du point de vue de l'expression.* The study of music history as a discipline had so little *droit de cité* at the Sorbonne that Rolland initiated the chair of musicology there in 1903 under the aegis of the department of history.

If *Les Origines du théâtre lyrique moderne* is not one of the monumental works of its field, it is still solid, based on careful study of historical documents, and obviously the work of a professional scholar as well as a profound lover of music. Its most original contribution to modern musicology is the discovery of Francesco Proven-

8. *In Cahiers Romain Rolland,* 9 (Paris, 1957).

zale, a Neapolitan master of the seventeenth century responsible for important innovations in opera and the teacher of Alessandro Scarlatti, among others.[9] Rolland's thesis is free of what might pass today for musical analysis: he limits himself by choice to biographical information, external events, plot summaries, and the like, with a minimal acknowledgment of the development of external and structural form. Most of his comments on the music itself have to do with its beauty, freshness, emotional and mimetic truth. But through the entire study there is a quality surprising in the first important published work of a young man of twenty-nine. It reflects a strong sense of intellectual and literary assurance and a wide-ranging grasp of historical and artistic context. One feels the presence of a historian who has established in his first work an original and personal point of view which his later works elaborate. This quality is evident from the first pages. In his introduction, Rolland outlines the ideas underlying his thesis, and one can see there the development of the philosophical precepts of *Credo quia verum* in the seven intervening years.

Rolland's predisposition to intuitive rather than logical cognition is manifest in certain prejudices of his method. His summary, indeed inadequate, treatment of formal aspects of the works studied proves to be a direct extension of this tendency to see a deeper truth in life than in form. Without denying the importance of new forms to reanimate the artistic experience of successive generations, he tends to see them as a function, a vehicle of the "genius" of great composers. Form in itself takes on a negative connotation, and it is only a composer's spirit which imbues the otherwise dead or inert form with creative life: "Enfin, quelques génies, recueillis et concentrés, donnent à la pensée de la race [italienne] son expression la plus profonde: le Romain Carissimi dans l'oratorio; Provenzale, de Naples, dans l'opéra." [10] He almost goes so far as to establish a conflict between form and content in his ensuing remarks. In the con-

---

9. Rolland is also credited with unearthing the manuscript of Luigi Rossi's *Orfeo* in the Chigi library in Rome and with demonstrating that this opera was given by Mazarin at the Palais-Royal in 1647. In general it may be said that Rolland is responsible to a great extent for the revival of interest in seventeenth-century opera in France.

10. *Origines,* p. 4.

text of historical development, Rolland's observations—or theory—lead him to note a negative correspondence between formal perfection and profound significance; that is to say, the arrival of a given formal configuration, such as opera or oratorio, at the moment of its greatest order, elegance, and symmetry seems to coincide with a moral and spiritual decadence, a "vide de la pensée." "La décadence des moeurs, l'affaiblissement de la personnalité, coïncidant avec les progrès purement extérieurs réalisés dans la musique, semblent faire de l'époque d'Alessandro Scarlatti, à la fois un sommet et un terme pour l'art." [11] Francesco Provenzale, on the other hand, in spite of formal imperfections, seems to Rolland a more profound master and the reflection of an era of constructive power.

Rolland tends to find two major forces at work, often in contradiction with each other, in the development of music during this period: the popular spirit which pervaded Italian opera, giving it its robust and contagious energy; and the increased reflection of personal sentiment, of psychological truth, which links this music across time with the development of opera in the nineteenth century. These two concepts which form an antiphonal chorus throughout all of Rolland's writings on music will be taken up in connection with *Jean-Christophe.*

It can be seen from the reference to Carissimi and Provenzale quoted above that Rolland laid heavy stress on the "racial" characteristics of art. In accordance with his idea of contagious life-force, he evolved a theory that moments of great creative energy in the history of a people create influential artistic forces which not only stimulate their own art but pass national frontiers and fertilize the creative process of other peoples. Thus the energy of the Italian "race" in music transmits itself during the latter half of the seventeenth century to France and Germany, which in turn become centers and propagators of operatic art. This cross-fertilization is an important aspect of the process of historical regeneration, which represents for Rolland the necessary movement of human life and art.

Rolland gives to the idea of cultural and artistic progress a defini-

11. Ibid., p. 5.

tion which is reminiscent of the peculiar understanding of that term Renan had suggested ten years before in an interview. Progress can be defined as a process of perfection, an accession toward ultimate, ideal Good, or as a movement toward identity with the spirit, with God. Both of these definitions presuppose a final cause toward which process tends and which represents the fulfillment that all preliminary stages have portended. But Roland refuses to see in artistic progress a necessary *improvement* of form or a perfection of the ideas to which forms give permanent shape. Elated with his discoveries of forgotten operas and other musical treasures, he finds the works of a more distant past as "perfect" in their genre, as true to the emotion from which they sprang, as more modern works.

Progress therefore represents for Rolland a catalytic agent by which the creative genius may find a fresh, effective way to express permanent ideas, sentiments, passions; it is not change toward a final perfection, but change for the sake of renovation.

> Il ne s'agit pas de penser des choses nouvelles; il s'agit d'être nouveau à les penser, d'apporter à sentir les vérités, qui sont le fonds commun des siècles, la sève d'une jeune nature qui ne les a pas encore vécues pour son compte et jouit passionnément de les éprouver en soi pour la première fois.[12]

The artist thus serves the function of renewing the creative outlets of human emotion; he is the intermediary between the experience of his era and the timeless current of human feelings.

The function of the historian, and especially the art historian, as conceived by Rolland is related to that of the creative artist. Through his intuitive penetration of spiritual and psychological movement in a period or nation, and through the unusually intimate and profound nature of the revelations furnished by the evidence of music and art, the art historian can give insights into the whys and hows of history which are not available to the political or social historian. He can report on the state of mind or of soul which produced the rise or decadence of a given people at a given time, or he can find currents which contrast with the visible evidence of events.

12. Ibid., p. 8.

Special training and inborn gifts are required to exploit his materials, but that does not invalidate or alter their usefulness. He can complete the understanding of humanity's past with information hitherto unavailable from neglected documents.

Rolland's conclusion to this introduction foretells the period of his *Beethoven* and *Jean-Christophe*. The theme of the "âmes souffrantes" already remarked in *Credo quia verum* is here extended to the musicologist's purpose: like the creative artist, the historian can act as an intermediary between man's present and past. The lessons of history, with its spectacle of constant regeneration, the transferal of active creation from generation to generation, race to race, can be an encouragement for future action, a remedy against pessimism and weariness. The author's almost unqualified optimism concerning the regeneration of art and the ability of man to penetrate the artistic spirit of past generations and profit by it is later tempered by doubt at several points in the unfolding of *Jean-Christophe*: Rolland tended increasingly to see this kind of appreciation as the privilege of an intellectual elite. But the aims and functions of art and art history outlined in his doctoral thesis remain surprisingly valid guidelines to his thought during the remainder of his career.

Rolland received his first real experience teaching during the three years preceding the acceptance of his doctoral thesis. He gave a complementary course in the history of art in the lycées of Paris (1893–94) and was a *professeur suppléant de morale* at the Ecole Jean-Baptiste Say (1895). Following the success of his thesis, which attracted attention in Paris and abroad, he was given a course to teach in the history of art at the Ecole Normale.[13] This first important professorial post in the history of art led, with Rolland's gradual specialization in musicology, to his nomination as director of the new school of music at the Ecole des Hautes Etudes Sociales in 1902 and to the first professorship in the history of music which was inaugurated at the Sorbonne in 1903.[14] According to the noted musi-

13. Péguy and Louis Gillet first came into contact with Rolland as students there, although Rolland and Péguy did not get to know each other until the latter undertook publication of Rolland's *Les Loups* in 1898.

14. A position which he held until his resignation from the teaching profession in 1912, when his associate André Pirro succeeded him.

cologist Henry Prunières, his success as a teacher was immense and directly attributable to his personal magnetism:

> Cinq cents personnes s'étouffaient chaque jeudi au cours de Romain Rolland à la Sorbonne pour l'entendre parler de Haendel, de Hasse, de Jomelli, il n'y en a pas cinquante aujourd'hui au cours pourtant d'une érudition incomparable de son successeur.[15]

Only Bergson's philosophy courses are said to have had a greater popularity at the time, a remarkable tribute to Rolland's gifts. In 1914, just before the outbreak of World War I, he had formed a small nucleus of musicological disciples as a result of his courses at the Sorbonne—Henry Prunières, Louis Laloy and Paul-Marie Masson—and had contributed to the popularization of the history of music by means of the course he founded at the Ecole des Hautes Etudes Sociales.

Rolland's inaugural lecture to the music school of the Ecole des Hautes Etudes Sociales, "De la place de la musique dans l'histoire générale," [16] is an extended statement of the views he advanced seven years earlier in the introduction to his thesis. He takes up again the special kind of knowledge available in musical documents: less clear and precise than literature, more difficult to analyze because of its irrationality and apparent abstraction from experience, but deeper and more intimate to the emotions and representative of a wider range of periods and regions, because of its ubiquity and universal language. He goes on to indicate its links with the other arts in the form of parallels, influences, exchanges, and collaborations (opera, for instance); but then he concentrates on the special knowledge music gives of the spiritual history of man.

> Mais à la prendre dans son essence même, son plus grand intérêt n'est-il pas de nous livrer l'expression toute pure de l'âme, les secrets de la vie intérieure, tout un monde de passions, qui

---

15. *Liber amicorum Romain Rolland* (Zurich and Leipzig, Rotapfelverlag, 1926), p. 294.

16. Published first in the *Revue d'Histoire et de Critique musicales* (June 1902), then in *Musiciens d'autrefois*.

> longuement s'amassent et fermentent dans le coeur, avant de
> surgir au grand jour? Souvent, grâce à sa profondeur et à sa
> spontanéité, la musique est le premier indice de tendances qui
> plus tard se traduisent en paroles, puis en faits.[17]

Thus music is privileged to give the nascent movements of history,
before their emergence in other forms. Tracing the history of music
in Europe, Rolland finds its evidence frequently in contradiction
with factual evidence: e.g. the rise of the Gregorian chant in the
context of the end of Rome and the barbarian invasions. Music is
the agent of continuity in human culture; like poetry, it is the art of
difficult times, of periods of withdrawal into the realm of the
spirit because of physical suffering or degeneration. Once again,
Rolland finds in the continuity of music and its constant shift from
country to country the moral comfort to which he referred in his
thesis:

> Le spectacle de cette éternelle floraison de la musique est un
> bienfait moral. C'est un repos au milieu de l'agitation uni-
> verselle. L'histoire politique et sociale est une lutte sans fin, une
> poussée de l'humanité vers un progrès constamment remis en
> question. . . . Mais de l'histoire artistique se dégage un ca-
> ractère de plénitude et de paix. Le progrès n'existe pas ici. Si
> loin que nous regardions derrière nous, la perfection a déjà été
> atteinte.[18]

Rolland's real effectiveness in the field of musicology, as might be
guessed from the popularity of his courses at the Sorbonne, seems
to have sprung more from his personality than from his discoveries.
It was partly, of course, a product of his method. The attempt to
seize the essence of a musical era through intuition of life and the
creative faculty gave his presentations an air of actuality. To Rolland, and therefore to his audience or reader, the music he was examining was not just an object of curiosity for the intellect; he was
concerned with the aesthetic and emotional impact of old music on
the modern listener. His method was to present the moral, spiritual,

17. *Musiciens d'autrefois*, pp. 4–5.
18. Ibid., p. 17.

and physical atmosphere of the era which produced the works, to make his public understand, or rather feel from within, the life of the composer and his public, for whom the music was new and fresh; and then to play examples of the music at the piano, while his audience was still in the spell of this evocation.

It must be remembered that this method required not only the gifts of intuition and presentation, but also the historiographical training which Rolland had received at the Ecole Normale and the Palais Farnèse. Even *Jean-Christophe* is much less a product of creative imagination than a large-scale synthesis of the historical and contemporary documentation which Rolland had spent his life amassing as a scholar and observer. It was this talent for synthesis which also gave his musicological efforts their special flavor. Rolland's incorporation of cultural history, as well as political, social, and intellectual history, set an example which was far-reaching in its effect.

The most individual contribution which Rolland made to the musical atmosphere of his time was a moral one. His ethical and moral approach to the study of music is to be found as much in his musicological works as in his novels and heroic biographies. The *Origines du théâtre lyrique,* carrying on the debate with Tolstoy, argues for the essential morality of opera against the critics it had since Boileau's attacks on the works and person of Lully. Rolland, like the author of *The Kreutzer Sonata* and *What Is Art?* underlines the dangers inherent in the "sublime passions of the noblest of musicians," Beethoven, when his art is absorbed by "mediocre spirits." But, like Tolstoy (although not with the same aesthetic criteria), Rolland considers that real operatic art, the art of Gluck and Beethoven, is not dangerous but wholesome. He takes Germany as the example of a country where music grew out of the "profound needs of the heart" and opera developed an entirely different character from what it had in France and Italy. He sees in German opera the elements of "spiritual grandeur and moral wholesomeness" that typify art which grows naturally out of popular expression.[19] It is on a similar basis that Rolland criticizes the Florentine

19. *Origines,* p. 13.

opera before Monteverdi: "Il était exclusivement princier; son aristocratique perfection l'éloignait de la vie commune et de l'âme populaire, sans laquelle on ne bâtit rien de fort." [20] Monteverdi brought to the composition of his music, perhaps for the first time in European history, the characteristic which was to become Rolland's rallying cry a decade later when his biographies were achieving their popularity: heroism. His definition of heroism is the personal one which has become connected with Rolland—greatness of heart and of faith (not in the orthodox sense necessarily), resistance to suffering and disappointment, participation in life-force and in nature, and an unvanquished spirit even in the face of the defeat which is the hero's lot.

Les Vies des hommes illustres: Beethoven

> L'air est lourd autour de nous. La vieille Europe s'engourdit dans une atmosphère pesante et viciée. Un matérialisme sans grandeur pèse sur la pensée, et entrave l'action des gouvernements et des individus. Le monde meurt d'asphyxie dans son égoïsme prudent et vil. Le monde étouffe.—Rouvrons les fenêtres. Faisons rentrer l'air libre. Respirons le souffle des héros.[21]

So opens the work of Romain Rolland which established his moral influence over his generation. It is impossible to treat *Beethoven* as musicology or music history, although Rolland deals in passing with the composer's principal works as landmarks or monuments in his life. The author was inspired by Plutarch and Carlyle, among others, to undertake a series of exemplary biographies, the *Vies des hommes illustres,* which would serve as an impulsion to hope and moral regeneration for his contemporaries. An ambitious and totally unrealistic list at the end of the volume promises seven studies to come: Hoche, Garibaldi, Thomas Paine, Mazzini, Michelangelo, Millet, and Schiller—a mixture of artistic and political figures which indicates the author's larger intentions. Only two of these saw print, Michelangelo and Millet (the latter in England);

20. Ibid., p. 83.
21. *Beethoven,* in *Cahiers de la Quinzaine,* p. 3.

Mazzini occupied Rolland's attention for several years. Two additional figures, Handel and Tolstoy, were eventually added to the list.

The importance of *Beethoven* as a spiritual event is reflected powerfully in Péguy's evaluation of its effect on his own moral and literary enterprise, the *Cahiers de la Quinzaine*. He indicates this clearly (if that word can be applied to his incantational oratory style) seven years later in his well-known essay *Notre Jeunesse:*

> Nos abonnés se rappellent encore quelle soudaine révélation fut ce cahier, quel émoi il souleva d'un bout à l'autre, comme il se répandit soudainement, comme une vague, comme en dessous, pour ainsi dire instantanément, comment il fut soudainement, instantanément, dans une révélation, aux yeux de tous, dans une entente soudaine, dans une commune entente, non point seulement le commencement de la fortune littéraire de Romain Rolland, et de la fortune littéraire des cahiers, mais infiniment plus qu'un commencement de fortune littéraire, une révélation morale, soudaine, un pressentiment dévoilé, révélé.[22]

In this slim volume—fifty pages of text, plus selected letters and the Heiligenstadt testament—Rolland pays moving tribute to his hero of heroes. Beethoven the composer is only incidental to Beethoven the moral giant; his music is seen as a function of his greatness of spirit:

> Cher Beethoven! Assez d'autres ont loué sa grandeur artistique. Mais il est bien davantage que le premier des musiciens. Il est la force la plus héroïque de l'art moderne. Il est le plus grand et le meilleur ami de ceux qui souffrent et qui luttent . . . . Il se dégage de lui une contagion de vaillance, un bonheur de la lutte, l'ivresse d'une conscience qui sent en elle un Dieu.[23]

In this monograph, heroic force and music are so intermingled as to become identified. Beethoven's music—that is, that part of his

---

22. *Cahiers de la Quinzaine*, Ser. 11, No. 12 (July 1910), p. 113.
23. *Beethoven*, pp. 52–53.

production which is the intimate reflection of his internal world—becomes a direct emanation of that force. Once again Rolland pays little attention to questions of form for their own sake, except to point out his hero's constant overstepping of formal restrictions, his redefinition of the limits of form. This is but one manifestation of Beethoven's heroic struggle. Rolland emphasizes the importance of the composer's sufferings: his loves, his material want during the last part of his life, his deafness, the public's incomprehension of his more advanced works, the ingratitude of his beloved nephew Karl. Beethoven becomes a great humanitarian, a social and political revolutionary, a scathing critic of his times. His march-like movements become "battle rhythms," his powerful middle period "this music of action and imperial triumphs." [24]

An echo of Rolland's idea that music completes and on occasion contradicts the visible evidence of history can be found in his account of the genesis of Beethoven's *Second Symphony*. Rolland sees it as an expression of the composer's will in its struggle with the depths of despondency into which his deafness had thrown him. "Une force irrésistible balaye les tristes pensées. Un bouillonnement de vie soulève le *finale*. Beethoven veut être heureux; il ne veut pas consentir à croire son infortune irrémédiable; il veut la guérison, il veut l'amour; il déborde d'espoir." [25] Such a demonstration of the triumph of will over adversity is calculated to instill courage into his readers, to demonstrate the extremities from which courage can snatch its victories *in the context of life and art,* not in the destructive battleground of military heroism. Beethoven becomes a model of heroism for everyday life.

Rolland's Beethoven draws his chief inspiration from the spectacle of nature. The author feels its presence, not only in such deliberately imitative works as the *Sixth Symphony* or the *"Pastoral" Sonata,* but in all the musical expressions of the composer's vital force:

> Il semble que dans sa communion de tous les instants avec la nature, il ait fini par s'en assimiler les énergies profondes . . . .
> Beethoven est une force de la nature; et c'est un spectacle d'une

24. Ibid., pp. 25–26.
25. Ibid., p. 23.

grandeur homérique, que ce combat d'une puissance élémen-
taire contre le reste de la nature.[26]

This communion with the external world makes Beethoven the ideal
embodiment of Rolland's formula, "Je sens, donc il Est." One can
see in him the significance of Rolland's introductory image of the
open window, an image which recurs frequently in his writing. The
window is a channel between the ego and all being, between the
imprisoned individual soul and the tremendous force of nature, between the victim of urban civilization and the sources of freedom.
Rolland, who had suffered since childhood from pulmonary dis-
orders, felt more powerfully than anyone the mediating force of
his composer-hero, who transported him to the open air, to the
forests and Alpine vistas he identified with freedom and life. His
debt of gratitude is paid in a work which is anything but a musicological treatise.

Rolland's Haendel

Romain Rolland's remaining works on music, during the period
preceding World War I, consist primarily of three volumes of essays
—*Musiciens d'autrefois* and *Musiciens d'aujourd'hui,* published in
1908, and *Voyage musical au pays du passé,* whose publication was
delayed by the war until 1919—and *Haendel,* which appeared in
1910.[27] The former consist of articles previously published in a
variety of journals, including the *Revue de Paris,* the *Mercure
musical,* the *Revue d'Histoire et de Critique musicales,* the *Revue
d'art dramatique,* and two German publications, *Morgen* and *Die
Musik.* Some of these essays, like the one on music history already
cited, and a few articles on the state of contemporary French music
—"*Pelléas et Mélisande* de Claude Debussy," "Musique française et
musique allemande," "Le Renouveau," in *Musiciens d'aujourd'hui*
—shed valuable light on the development of Rolland's musical ideas,
especially his nationalism, in the period immediately preceding the
publication of *Jean-Christophe,* and interesting contrasts in the

26. Ibid., p. 53.
27. *Musiciens d'autrefois* and *Musiciens d'aujourd'hui* were published in Paris by
Hachette; *Haendel,* in Paris by Félix Alcan.

nuances of his opinion can be had by confronting articles and novel. In general, however, their interest is journalistic and anecdotal, and the limitations of Rolland's aims and public show clearly.

Haendel is another question entirely. It is far from having the moral weight and significance of *Beethoven,* which is a unique phenomenon. For one thing, it does not reflect so troubled a period of Rolland's life as the earlier volume, which the author described as having emerged from dual catastrophes in his life: the death of the dear friend of his youthful years in Rome, Malwida von Meysenbug, and his divorce from Clotilde Bréal after ten years of marriage. For another, Rolland's literary reputation was established, and he was still occupied in an absorbing task, the completion of *Jean-Christophe,* which, along with his academic responsibilities, gave an increased stability to his life.

The personal importance of *Haendel* must not be underestimated, however. It is different from the emotional and moral function of *Beethoven.* Handel the composer represented for Rolland a kind of health cure, an exposure to wholesome, vigorous genius that counterbalanced some of the pathetic, troubled elements connected with Beethoven's heroism. As early as 1890, a letter to his mother from Rome bears witness to this "hygienic" function Handel exercised in Rolland's life: "Je me nourris de Handel. C'est comme du rosbif saignant. C'est sain, robuste et fortifiant." [28] As in the case of Goethe, whom the younger Rolland disdained for his apparent inhuman equilibrium, this response is oversimplified when compared to the portrait of Handel which emerged from Rolland's maturity. But then his appreciation was to be nuanced rather than essentially altered.

A letter to Sofia Bertolini in 1908 indicates the increased complexity of Rolland's idea of Handel during the period of his preparation of the book.

> "Voici la deuxième année que je passe à étudier Haendel. Je
> joue en moyenne une ou deux oeuvres nouvelles de lui, par
> semaine . . . . C'est tout un univers. Et dans ce monde de chefs

28. *Retour au Palais Farnèse,* p. 125.

d'oeuvre, il y a les plus belles tragédies grecques que l'on ait faites depuis Sophocle, et la plus magnifique musique de plein air, que l'on ait écrite pour tout un peuple." [29]

It is obvious that Handel was preoccupying Rolland's attention to the detriment of his other favorites, including Beethoven, and this shift in attention is evident in the volumes of *Jean-Christophe* written during this period. Handel was no longer for Rolland simply the wholesome "rare roastbeef" of musical history. The composer's complexity fascinated him as Goethe's would later, reflecting the author's own desire to avoid definition: "Il n'est pas de grand musicien qu'il soit aussi impossible que Haendel d'enfermer dans une définition, ou même dans plusieurs." [30] Even more than Beethoven, Handel seemed to Rolland "a force of nature," the creative genius turned outward, open to the external world. His instrumental music reflected not just his personal universe: "Elle est aussi tournée vers le spectacle des choses. Elle est une poésie précise." [31] He seemed the type of the "objective bard" that Rolland was seeking in his new art.[32]

Part of this outside world for Handel was the life and art of the people. "Il allait boire . . . aux ruisseaux de musique populaire, aux plus simples, aux plus rustiques. Il les aimait." [33] In a period when Rolland was increasingly conscious of the need for a truly popular art, Beethoven's music seemed too limited in its appeal, too much an art of the elite. Handel's work was less intimately related to the personality and struggles of its creator, less an emanation of his passions and bitterness. It was objective, written not to express the composer's soul but to stir and to please a large audience:

> Ce que j'entends par le caractère populaire de la musique de Haendel, c'est qu'elle est vraiment conçue pour tout un peuple, et non pour une élite de dilettantes . . . . Notre époque a perdu le sens de ce type d'art et d'hommes: de purs artistes qui parlent

29. *Chère Sophia, 1,* 378.
30. *Haendel,* p. 137.
31. Ibid., p. 178.
32. See *Jean Christophe,* pp. 1174–78.
33. *Haendel,* p. 141.

au peuple et pour le peuple, non pour eux seuls et pour quelques confrères.[34]

This was doubly "outdoor music": suited by its healthy aggressiveness for outdoor performance to large audiences, it breathed the epic power of nature and life-force upon its listeners.

The popular character of Handel's music became for Rolland a political and geographical universality, which he admired at this stage of his ideological development. Handel scorned the limitations of nationalism: "De patriotisme allemand, il n'en avait guère. Il avait la mentalité des grands artistes allemands de son temps, pour qui la patrie, c'était l'art et la foi. Peu lui importait l'Etat." [35] His music, viewed as a body, reflects the travels and displacements of his life. In style as well as language, his operas and oratorios show the influence of those countries in which he studied and resided: Germany, Italy, England. Handel's peculiar genius lies in his mastery of all styles and forms, but the genre in which he excelled, the oratorio, was the popular form par excellence, designed to instill a great audience with pride in its spiritual heritage by use of massive forces and monolithic structures. Handel's treatment of Old Testament subjects represented to Rolland, not a narrow reflection of Protestant English tastes, but an effort to find a common traditional ground, to speak in the language of all men: "Ce n'est pas dans une pensée religieuse que Haendel a fait choix, pour une partie d'entre eux, de sujets bibliques, mais . . . parce que les histoires des héros bibliques étaient entrées dans le sang du peuple, à qui il voulait parler." [36]

As a composer of full-bodied epic works for mass audiences, Handel seemed to Rolland a valuable corrective to the potentially dangerous subjective power of Beethoven. This ideologically directed taste never succeeded in displacing Rolland's earlier passion, as the later extensive studies of Beethoven testify. But there is an important period, during the writing of *Jean-Christophe,* when Rolland came close to building an entirely new ideal of music on the heroic model provided by Handel.

34. Ibid., p. 234.
35. Ibid., p. 83.
36. Ibid., p. 166.

The Function of Music in Rolland's Thought

The preceding pages give an idea of the important role that music played in Romain Rolland's life and of the equally important one that the author played in the musical life of his time. But the writings and events referred to do not come close to measuring the full extent of music's presence in his daily life and intellectual and professional endeavors. Rolland was a devoted and gifted piano player; an inveterate reader of scores and concert-goer; a conversationalist for whom music was a privileged subject; the friend of such musicians as Richard Strauss, Ernest Bloch, Maurice Ravel, and Edgar Varèse; the promoter or "protector" of Dom Lorenzo Perosi, Paul Dupin, and, posthumously, of the reputation of Hugo Wolf; a tireless organizer of concerts and participant in musical congresses; and a collaborator in musical encyclopedias. The list is still far from complete and indicates only the quality and variety of his commitment to the field of music, not the quantity and degree to which he was engaged in it.

The astonishing thing, to anyone looking at his bibliography and surveying the events of his life, is that Rolland found time to engage so extensively in the number of nonmusical interests with which his name is identified: civil liberties, political manifestations, internationalism and world peace, the emancipation of women, East-West relations, Russian and German literature, Italian culture and politics, and so on. His nonmusical literary works include numerous plays, several novels, biographies of Michelangelo, Tolstoy, Gandhi, Ramakrishna, Vivekananda, and Péguy, numerous political and literary essays, and a voluminous correspondence and spiritual diary (a great deal of it as yet unpublished in spite of the tireless efforts of his widow and admirers).

But although music in its various forms had to share the numerous chambers of Rolland's mind with his other passionate interests, it still occupied a central place, *the* central place, in his affections; and its influence can be felt in all areas of Rolland's thought. This is true not only in the external sense, in the overt or implied references to music which can be found in all contexts of his work; but also, more importantly still, in his very manner and style of thinking, in the patterns of the analogies and metaphors which his thought and writing takes. It will be our task in a concluding chapter to this study to define the intrinsically musical quality in the construction of *Jean-Christophe*. For the moment we will define some of the elementary thought patterns which dominate Rolland's writing in general and see in what ways they reflect the constant companionship of music, indeed his immersion in it from the early years of his life.

It is not within the scope of this study to examine all the influences to which Romain Rolland's concept of music can be traced. In a certain sense, of course, Rolland as a great synthesizer of ideas must be seen as the apex of a historical pyramid, at whose base are found the pre-Socratic philosophers and Oriental mystics, and close to the top, the German Romantics, Schopenhauer, Nietzsche, and, side-by-side with Rolland, Henri Bergson. Some of the elements of this pyramid would have direct connections with Rolland's thought, but most of them, indeed some of the most apparently apt ones, would be linked to him only by coincidence or very indirect influence.[37]

If Rolland's mode of thought is to be characterized as reflecting the importance of music in his life, it is necessary to define what is characteristic of musical, as opposed to literary or artistic, experience and what the laws of musical structure are, as opposed to other intellectual or artistic structures. We will first define these briefly, in a tentative way, and then develop more extensively, from an examination of some of Rolland's dominant metaphorical patterns, what there is in them which is analogous to musical experience and structure.

A little volume has appeared recently, containing a series of conversations on music between the noted conductor Ernest Ansermet and a young philosopher friend.[38] Near the end of the series, Ansermet finally attempts to define what music is, after long and circumstantial reflections on its history and practice. This attempt at defi-

37. René Cheval has demonstrated, for example, the limitations of Rolland's contact with German literature of the nineteenth century during his formative period. See his excellent study, *Romain Rolland, l'Allemagne et la guerre*.

38. E. Ansermet and J.–C. Piguet, *Entretiens sur la musique;* transcripts of broadcasts by Radio Genève in the winter of 1961–62.

nition, based on the experience of a long and honored career as well
as the meditations of a lucid intellect, bears striking relevance to
patterns of Rolland's thought and may help to *define* its musicality
better than reference to the philosophical tradition which influenced
its shaping. It has the incidental advantage of being the explanation
of a musician rather than a philosopher.

In answer to the voluntarily bald question of his interlocutor,
"What is music?" Ansermet replies:

> Elle est sentiment en acte et du sentiment signifié par son image
> sensible, comme notre langage est de la pensée signifiée par des
> locutions verbales, des mots et des phrases, en sorte que l'image
> mélodique telle qu'elle se déploie dans le temps est un langage,
> mais un langage sans concept et purement affectif.[39]

Music, like all the arts, is sentiment or the translation of sentiment;
but unlike literature it is a translation by means of sense images
which directly represent sentiment, rather than by means of words
or signs which represent concepts, which in turn represent or evoke
sentiments. It is therefore more immediate as experience than literary art, and less intellectual. Indeed, Ansermet goes on to insist that
music does not simply represent sentiments, but that music is itself
a human sentiment *sui-generis* and exists as such without necessary
reference to other nonmusical sentiments. The particular human
sentiment which music reveals or manifests is a primal state of
psychic existence preceding intellectual cognition (the coincidence
with Rolland's *Credo quia verum* is evident here). Ansermet once
again underlines the immediacy of music to human experience, as
compared to linguistic media of expression:

> Le sentiment nous parle de l'homme et il ne faut pas dire . . .
> que la musique est expression de sentiments, mais qu'elle est
> une expression de l'homme par ses modalités de sentiments, ce
> qui lui confère une transcendance de signification qui doit nous
> la faire prendre au sérieux et qui fait toute la valeur de son
> témoignage. Mais elle ne nous révèle de l'homme . . . que son
> être psychique, et les modalités de son être psychique qui est son

39. Ibid., p. 144.

être caché antérieur au *cogito* et pourtant source de ses déter-
minations fondamentales.[40]

The transcendent element of music, then, lies in its being not an
expression of human sentiments but, immediately, an expression of
man by his sentiments. Its peculiar value is that it is a plane of con-
juncture between the internal world of man and the physical world:
what Karl Feininger called "the immortal calculus under which
internality and externality can be made to appear *enharmoni-
ously.*"[41]

The peculiar fact of musical experience, which distinguishes it
from other forms of expression, is the importance of time. All
aesthetic experience is of course based on the relationship of the consciousness, through the senses, with the space-time continuum.
"Was zur Empfindung kommt, sind Gebilde, die sich in Raum und
Zeit erstrecken" is the beginning of an encyclopedia definition of
the musical experience which could be applied to the other arts as
well.[42] But whereas in visual art the time factor is traditionally
minimized or even negated, and in literature both space and time
are made relative by the intermediary function of the printed page,
in music the space factor is relegated to secondary importance or
less, and time becomes an almost absolute modality of expression
and existence. For music really exists only in the context of time
(the score being merely a conventional system of signs to approxi-
mate and preserve the original temporal experience). Participation
in musical experience requires of both performer and audience a
total identification of their existence, their internal time, with the
time (in all the senses of the word) of the music. Therefore the
work of music has existence by the medium of the time-experience
of its listeners, who confer upon it the totality of the psychic activity; at the same time, however, the work of music exists as a self-
contained unit, an entity and totality which has its beginning and
end, its necessary movement and division. As Ansermet states:

40. Ibid., p. 145.
41. *An Experiential Psychology of Music* (New York, 1909), p. 254.
42. *Die Musik in Geschichte und Gegenwart* (12 vols. Kassel, Bärenreiter-Verlag,
1949–63), 9, 959.

L'acte d'existence musicale, c'est-à-dire ce que nous vivons à l'écoute d'une oeuvre musicale, a un commencement et une fin, et ne prend le sens d'un acte d'existence accompli, noué et dénoué, clos sur lui-même et ayant en lui-même son propre fondement que s'il est fondé sur la structure tonique-dominante-tonique . . . . Or qu'est-ce que cette structure, sinon le mode qu'a la conscience musicale de se signifier dans la transcendance de son chemin mélodique la structure passé-présent-futur, c'est-à-dire la structure par laquelle s'annonce, au coeur de l'homme, le mode d'être de Dieu, le Logos divin? [43]

The peculiar mode of existence of the work of music may therefore be summarized as follows:

1º Its direct expression of the internal world of man, not as an intellectual cognition, but through the sentiments themselves and as pure sentiment

2º Its primary expression of the temporal, durational experience of man, which is his deepest, most primitive mode of knowledge of existence; and conversely, its existence as an art form only in the context of internal and external time, which it conjoins and which is, in its aspects of duration, measure, and rhythm, the modality of its existence

3º Its motive structure, within the absolute unity of its temporal existence, based on the alternation of tonic-dominant-tonic, that is to say of cadence and the resolution of dissonance

When the attentive reader of *Jean-Christophe* confronts the novel with Rolland's other writings, he is struck by certain insistent recurring patterns in the author's thought which are not, strictly speaking, logical. What is striking about them is that they seem to be sentiments of movement rather than intellectual or analytical processes. While they resemble such traditional patterns of thought as intuition and dialectic, they seem to be rather the "image" of these processes. Their primary reality is felt to be in the primitive sense of movement through time and space, which is the core of musical sentiment.

43. *Entretiens*, pp. 150–51.

There are three principal formal manifestations which this sentiment of movement takes in Rolland's thought patterns. Each one
plays a prominent role in the formulation and expression of his concept of human nature and experience, especially that of the
musician-hero, Jean-Christophe, who is a literary synthesis of Rolland's ideas. Taken together as dominant psychic laws in the psychological structure of the hero, they complement and correct each
other, alternately and simultaneously, so as to be shaped into a
varied and shifting equilibrium of movement and stasis. Each of
these patterns or laws has a particular archetypal image attached to
it which contributes to the metaphoric structure of Rolland's novel
in a way resembling poetic or musical motive—leitmotiv—rather
than novelistic technique. But since these three patterns are so
basic to all of Rolland's thought, they should be considered less in
terms of literary or artistic procedure than as a musical pattern of
thinking which habitually finds verbal expression in motive images
directly expressing a state of sentiment.

The first of these habits is that of conceiving human life and
psychic activity, at its most basic level, in terms of *duration*. Roland
in his early notes refers to this obsessive pattern, which is certainly
the original and most durable facet of his thought. One example
will suffice here, a note in his diary at the Ecole Normale. Speaking
of his desire to write the "histoire des âmes" referred to above, Rolland writes: "Ce sera une oeuvre longue: car je ne sais pas voir une
âme, en un moment précis, isolé, de son existence; je ne la vois que
dans la suite de son évolution." [44] His basic idea of psychology is
to attune himself to the personality being studied (if that verb may
be applied here) and to attempt to live in at least an approximation
of the sentiment of duration which is the other's. Similarly, in
creating his fictional personality, Jean-Christophe, Rolland accepts
the absolute necessity of following the evolution of his life from
birth to death. The dominant image which represents this particular pattern of psychic movement is that of the *river:* the succeeding chapter will show its primary connection in Rolland's thought
with the ideas of Spinoza.

44. *Cloître*, p. 189.

A second psychological and creative pattern, which completes and corrects the first one, is the prevailing movement of *alternation*. It is a corrective in that it gives shape, rhythm, and direction to the otherwise monotonous flow of the river. Fittingly enough, it takes on its archetypal shape not in the liquid element of undifferentiated substance in water, but first of all in a geometric form-in-motion, the *spiral,* and second in an image of rocklike hardness and human effort, the *"route en lacets qui monte."* Rolland tended to mingle this motive theme, whose formulation he drew from an early conversation with Renan, with another pattern, "Death and Becoming"—"Stirb und werde"—which he owed to his later appreciation of Goethe. Both of these movements, in their primary emphasis on change through alternation as a means of progression toward a transcendent goal, are analogous to the alternation of dissonance and resolution which is the rhythmic, metric, dynamic basis of movement within the unity of the musical work.

The final psychic pattern which dominates Rolland's writing is represented metaphorically by the *house.* The image of the house, traditionally suggesting stability and enclosure, would seem to be antithetical to the idea of movement. But this image, which gives its structure to one of the central volumes of Rolland's novel (*Dans la Maison*), takes on an active life of its own in his work. Like the mountain road, the house represents a kind of alternation within the evolutionary stream of consciousness, but it is an ethical and psychological one within the mind of the author. The house represents, through its internal opposition of unity and multiplicity (the building and its rooms united and yet separate: Rolland's house is, of course, the Parisian *immeuble*), the alternating self-contained unity of the ego and its identity with the all-soul and the rest of humanity. The house embodies the shifting of Rolland's spiritual identity between the sense of personal duration, of individual life-force in its internal evolution, and the sense of belonging to the collective destiny of mankind. This dialogue is a constant phenomenon of Rolland's psychology and can be most closely identified, through a series of "éclairs" which broke the sense of spiritual imprisonment, with the influence of Leo Tolstoy.

II. SPINOZA, RENAN, GOETHE: THE
PATTERN OF CREATIVE BECOMING

Spinoza: The River of Becoming

Romain Rolland attributes the germinal inspiration of his *Jean-Christophe* to a vision which came to him on the Janicular Hill in Rome, in March of 1890.[1] Typically, Rolland describes this "revelation" in the intuitional analogies which characterize his writing when he is dealing with the profound roots of creation and life. Rather than an idea in the literary sense or an architecture, this first seed of creation seems to have been a flash of light illuminating the horizons of his imagination, an intuition of the course to be followed by the hero to come. Rolland's difficulty in transcribing the revelation is not surprising if one takes into account the nature of the novel which grew out of it during the next twenty-two years. The revelation itself seems a metaphor of that intuition which was to be the true form of his novel. "Ce qu'en cette seconde j'ai embrassé du regard, je n'aurais pu en dessiner les traits; mais par la suite, au long de mon chemin, que de fois je les ai reconnus!"[2]

One must of course use caution in accepting the testimony which Rolland noted almost fifty years later. The events of intervening years, especially such a dominant event as *Jean-Christophe,* tend to reshape memory in regard to such tenuous things as origins. But the notes and letters on which Rolland was basing his memoirs substantiate his literary reconstruction. *Jean-Christophe* owes its initial impulsion to a vision of the Roman campagna, transformed by the setting sun into "a sea,"[3] into which Rolland felt himself being

---

1. *Mémoires,* pp. 103–04. The experience took place during Rolland's first year at the Palais Farnèse.
2. Ibid., p. 104.
3. Ibid., p. 103.

absorbed. The welding of this metaphor of all-being with the road, which Rolland felt was the necessary image of the movement of life in its external manifestations, gave birth, implicitly at least, to the dominant image of his novel, the river.

It is true, as René Cheval claims, that the external form, the identity of Jean-Christophe's "river of life," came out of Rolland's later visit to Mainz in 1896 and the impression the Rhine made on him then.[4] That was six years after the initial vision of his novel, however. Indeed a deeper and more primitive impulsion to use the river as a dominant metaphor comes from Rolland's memories of his home in Clamecy: numerous references to his native town dwell on the canal in which his house was reflected. The Rhine, of course, has suggestive resonances of great importance to *Jean-Christophe*: its connection with Bonn and Beethoven, its identity as a European river, its active role as the artery of life for the regions it links through commerce and communication. But the intimate relationship between Rolland's concept of internal life-force, the architecture of his novel, and the metaphor of the river is defined years before the "revelation" of the Rhine in 1896.[5]

Rolland indicates in his *Mémoires* that the birth of his hero and of the new kind of novel were not precisely simultaneous. According to his chronology, based on letters and notes of the period, the experience of the Janicular Hill was essentially a spiritual one, a vision of life-force and its manifestation in the hero's personality. The concept of the "musical" novel, emerging in the period immediately following, for a time existed independently of the other inspiration. Yet it is apparent that this new literary form was inseparable from Rolland's spiritual vision; it can be called, in literary terms, an architectural "figure" of the metaphysical truth the author had glimpsed. The basic idea of the musical novel, quoted by Rolland from a letter to Malwida von Meysenbug, reveals this clearly: "Toutes les parties en seraient issues d'un même thème

---

4. *Romain Rolland, l'Allemagne et la guerre*, p. 87.

5. Rolland had seen the Rhine for the first time in 1887, *before* the experience of the Janicular Hill, but at that time he noted a keen disappointment of his expectations. The river metaphor, therefore, might be said to emerge *in spite of* the image of the Rhine which he then had. See Cheval, p. 85.

général et puissant, à la façon d'une symphonie, bâtie sur quelques notes exprimant un sentiment, qui se développe en tous les sens, grandit, triomphe, ou succombe, au cours de l'oeuvre." Rolland hastens to add (fifty years later): "Le mot de fleuve n'y est point inscrit. Mais est-ce autre chose, une symphonie?"[6] Thus the analogical connection between music (as well as the musician-hero) and the river, if one is to believe Rolland's later commentary, was already clearly foreshadowed in August 1890, the date of Rolland's letter to Malwida von Meysenbug.[7]

In its primitive form, however, the river metaphor was not yet clearly defined and delimited, or rather, it had a different shape which required the action of a more defined force to transform it into the river. In the beginning, the metaphoric representation of being which dominated Rolland's sentiments was the *ocean,* the unlimited expanse of liquid substance engulfing the myriad elements of its composition in a unity suggestive of infinity. The *Credo quia verum* and Rolland's philosophical notes during the years at the Ecole Normale make frequent use of the ocean metaphor to represent the individual being's relation with the infinity of being.

The initial intuition of being, the soul's first sentiment of existence which establishes the axiom "Je sens, donc Il Est," is expressed by Rolland in terms of liquid metaphors whose unstable variety testifies to the early part they played in his development of the river image:

> Dans la nuit silencieuse de mon être, un flot régulier passe; et son bruissement monte jusqu'à moi, comme le chant monotone du ruisseau que le meunier n'entend plus, parce qu'il n'a pas de fin. C'est un flot sur qui danse un instant un rayon de lumière, et qui fuit aussitôt dans l'ombre inconnue. Un flot de nuages brillants ou sombres, qui glissent sur le ciel et se fondent sans bruit. Un flot de sensations, d'images et d'idées, qui coule intarissable et ne revient jamais.—Arrêtons au passage quelques gouttes du courant.[8]

6. *Mémoires,* p. 104.
7. *Choix de lettres à Malwida von Meysenbug,* p. 26.
8. *Cloître,* p. 358.

The growing intuition of being which comes from the sense of duration, the temporal continuity and identity of the individual, is also expressed in an ocean image: "Milliards de sensations, gouttelettes qui grossissent, se resserrent, disparaissent, pour revenir de nouveau à la surface de l'Océan de l'Etre." [9] The identity of the individual soul with the all-soul also finds expression in this image of unity and multiplicity: "l'Océan innombrable et la paix éternelle de ses agitations sans fin." [10]

Even at this stage of its development, the liquid metaphor is clearly linked with music, especially the symphonic structure to which Rolland's later letter refers: "Comparons Dieu à un artiste qui écoute une phrase musicale qu'il se chante à lui-même. Chaque note de cette phrase est une sensation du Moi divin. Romain Rolland est un groupe de sensations, un accord." [11] But this conception of the nature of symphonic structure based on the triple analogy of ocean, music, and all-being is incomplete compared with what it becomes in the complex interaction of forces underlying *Jean-Christophe*. Its very incompleteness testifies to the primary source of this metaphor and the concept it embodies in Rolland's thought: Spinoza. Quoting from a letter to Suarès, his friend and contemporary at the Ecole Normale, Rolland points out that, until he injects the idea of "rôles" as a stopgap measure, the ingredient missing from his tentative credo is action; that is precisely, in his view, the failing of his philosophical inspiration, "le Spinozisme." [12] The major difference Rolland finds between his personal philosophical system and the synthesis of Spinoza's thought from which he derived it is freedom of action, a place for individual liberty: "Le sage n'est pas celui qui s'absorbe en Dieu, mais qui, sachant être Dieu, joue son rôle, avec une paix passionnée." [13]

It can thus be stated that, even at this early stage in Rolland's conception of the creative life and its literary manifestation, the *modalities*—the vectors of forces and counterforces—are in the

9. Ibid., p. 360.
10. Ibid., p. 361.
11. Ibid., p. 366.
12. Ibid., p. 81.
13. Ibid., p. 88.

process of being defined by influences outside Spinoza: primarily
Renan and Tolstoy. But the *substance* of the river is essentially the
metaphorical analogue of ideas—or rather sentiments—derived from
Rolland's experience in reading Spinoza a few years before the
formulation of *Credo quia verum.*

The "éclair de Spinoza" was the second in time of the "three
flashes" which Rolland describes in his *Voyage intérieur.* The first,
the least literarily defined, was a revelation of nature which came
to him for a brief instant, at the age of sixteen, on the terrace at
Ferney. This experience, unrelated to the souvenirs of Voltaire
connected with the place, Rolland describes as a kind of possession
of his soul, "vierge violée," by the landscape, the first of his powerful reactions to nature. It can be taken as the initiation of his
tendency to feel an immanent divinity in the visible world and to
associate extended vistas with spiritual vision. The sensual introduction to pantheism obviously was an important preparation for
the intellectual "flashes" to come and for what Rolland was to
call his "artistic pantheism." [14]

Rolland dwells in much greater detail on the revelation of Spinoza in his *Voyage intérieur.* Completing the vision of Ferney, it
was more clearly defined, for an intellectual spirit, by the setting
in which it took place: the room in which Rolland spent his days
and nights preparing the entrance examinations for the Ecole Normale. The author was nineteen years old, "walled up" in a room
overlooking the rue Michelet and the garden of the Ecole de Phar-
macie. He considered himself a prisoner of necessity, a victim of
the educational machine. Into this "cell," suddenly, through the
reading of a few pages of a book, burst a vision of the "gouffre de la
Substance . . . le soleil blanc de l'Etre." [15] The revelation seemed
to open out the walls of his room and of his individuality. Rolland
describes the scene in emotional terms which testify to the enduring
power of the revelation. He cites with filial gratitude the edition
in which he had discovered the philosopher [16] and indicates specific

14. Ibid., p. 249.
15. *Voyage intérieur*, p. 45.
16. Emile Saisset's translation of B. Spinoza, *Oeuvres de Spinoza*, first published
in 1844, which Rolland read in the revised edition of 1872.

passages in the text which effected this transformation in his life: primarily Definitions 3, 4, 5, and 6, and the Explanation following them in Part I of the *Ethics;* and Propositions 15 and 16 of Part I, and the *Scholie* of *Lemma* 7 in Part II, for a few "étincelles." The Definitions seem cold material for such emotional response:

III. J'entends par *substance* ce qui est en soi et est conçu par soi, c'est-à-dire ce dont le concept peut être formé sans avoir besoin du concept d'une autre chose.

IV. J'entends par *attribut* ce que la raison conçoit dans la substance comme constituant son essence.

V. J'entends par *mode* les affections de la substance, ou ce qui est dans autre chose, et est conçu par cette même chose.

VI. J'entends par *Dieu* un être absolument infini, c'est-à-dire une substance constituée par une infinité d'attributs dont chacun exprime une essence éternelle et infinie.

EXPLICATION. Je dis absolument infini, et non pas infini en son genre; car toute chose qui est infinie seulement en son genre, on en peut nier une infinité d'attributs; mais, quant à l'être absolument infini, tout ce qui exprime une essence et n'enveloppe aucune négation, appartient à son essence.[17]

The impression which this passage made on the adolescent Rolland must be examined within the frame of reference of the mind which was absorbing it; he admits to the importance of a factor extraneous to the text: "Dans l'inscription tracée au porche de l'*Ethique,* dans ces *Définitions* aux lettres flamboyantes, je déchiffrais, non ce qu'il avait dit, mais ce que je voulais dire, les mots que ma propre pensée d'enfant, de sa langue inarticulée, s'évertuait à épeler." [18] He sees in Spinoza and in these definitions, not the rationalist, "the master of geometric order" who concealed his real nature and his most powerful innovations under the "weighty intellectual verbalism of professional philosophers," but the realist. The definitions must be understood by cross-reference to the *Treatise on Understanding:* " 'Il est absolument nécessaire de tirer

17. Ibid., 2, 5.
18. *Voyage intérieur*, p. 42.

toutes nos idées des choses physiques, c'est-à-dire des êtres réels, en allant, suivant la série des causes, d'un être réel à un autre être réel, sans passer aux choses abstraites et universelles.' " [19]

This revealed to Rolland that the laws governing existence were inherent in reality and that man, too, lived by laws of internal necessity, which were part of his substance. There was no need to refer to causes outside of nature: the understanding of human nature, for example, depended on the penetration of "life," the internal force which was the sum of the attributes of Being. Rolland seized on Spinoza's statement that "everything that is, is in God"; since "Nature naturante" and "Nature naturée" were the same thing, every being, inasmuch as he partook of and participated in the nature of God, was at the same time created and creator. Rolland derived from this the individual's submersion in the "gouffre de *la Substance* . . . le soleil blanc de l'Etre" and his liberty to fulfill a law which he both received and created. It is evident that Rolland was interested not in the strict rational order of proof which forms the architecture of the *Ethics,* but rather in a synthesis of those parts which accorded with previously half-formulated views of man and nature. Spinoza gave him a first glimpse of that combination of mysticism and action which was to form the dual nature of the Rollandian hero, especially the heroic creative artist, Jean-Christophe.

The experience of Spinoza through an intuitional rather than an analytic understanding of some of his writings can be taken in itself as a "figure" of the experiential reality revealed to Rolland. That is to say, Rolland's discovery of himself in Spinoza's philosophic treatise was based on an intuited sense of his identity with the author and, by extension, with all of creation. This seems to have been Rolland's first powerful contact with this kind of nonrational subjective cognition, across time and space, through literature— or at least it remained marked in his mind as such. It was, however, a technique which he was to carry to considerable lengths later:

19. *Treatise on Understanding,* cited in *Voyage intérieur,* pp. 43–44.

On se lit à travers les livres, soit pour se découvrir, soit pour se contrôler. Et les plus objectifs sont les plus illusionnés. Le plus grand livre n'est pas celui dont le communiqué s'imprimerait au cerveau . . . mais celui dont le choc vital éveille d'autres vues et de l'une à l'autre propage son feu qui s'alimente des essences diverses." [20]

Thus in this experience can be seen the germ of his ideas on the "histoire des âmes," leading ultimately to the technique of historical analysis through music.

Rolland's poetic representation of the discovery of Spinoza, as he lived it during his eighteenth year, is dominated by images of space, of light, which combine the experience of spiritual revelation with a sense of physical immensity and freedom, contrasting with the confines of his room. The following paragraph illustrates how the elements of freedom, infinity, multiplicity, and illumination combined to form the ocean image which embodies Spinoza's ideas for Rolland:

Horizons inouïs! Mon rêve, même en ses vols les plus délirants, est dépassé. Non seulement mon corps et mon esprit, mon univers, baignent dans des mers sans rivages, l'Etendue, la Pensée, dont nulle caravelle ne pourra faire le tour. Mais dans l'insondable immensité, j'entends bruire, à l'infini, d'autres mers, d'autres mers inconnues, des Attributs innombrables, inconcevables, à l'infini. Et tous sont contenus en l'Océan de l'Etre. [21]

The transformation of this metaphoric representation of internal life and its communication with all-being from the limitless, unshaped ocean to the combined absorbency and direction of the river is evidently a process which took place during the period between Rolland's flash of revelation while reading Spinoza and the composition of the first scene in *L'Aube*. Already, at the end of his diary at the Ecole Normale, there is a first example of the change

20. *Voyage intérieur,* p. 43.
21. Ibid., p. 45.

when Rolland talks of death as the "confluence of the individual soul with the infinite river." [22] One is tempted by the context of this passage to indulge in conjecture: Rolland, after his long period of enforced contemplative activity—or inactivity—had just passed his *agrégation d'histoire* and was on the brink of commitment to an active career in the world outside. For the first time, he is forced to see his life in terms of a direction, not just theoretically, but practically. During the years separating Rolland's meditation in the "Cloître" from the opening of *Jean-Christophe,* the river took shape, so to speak, underground, hidden by professional preoccupations and the ten-year interruption by his theatrical ambitions. The experience of the Rhine in 1896, cited by Cheval, is a momentary emergence of the theme into Rolland's writings, but it remained dormant, although it was gradually taking form, until its appearance in the first volume of the novel. There it organically takes shape, is actively transformed from the featureless sea of all-being into the river of the heroic personality during the first half of *L'Aube.*

The apparent echo of Bergson's thought which is found in this conception of duration and cognition is a striking example of coincidence or zeitgeist at work. Describing the effect of Bergsonian intuitionism on his former associate Péguy's generation at the turn of the century, Rolland recognized the resemblance between his idea of history and human understanding and Bergson's. Near the end of his life, in his biography of Péguy, he cites a passage from *L'Introduction à la métaphysique,* first published in the *Cahiers* in 1903, which sounds like a paraphrase of views he had expressed in his diary of the Ecole Normale:

> La science moderne date du jour où l'on érigea la mobilité en réalité indépendante . . . . Et philosopher consiste à se placer, par un effort d'intuition, à l'intérieur de cette réalité concrète . . . . Les grandes découvertes sont des coups de sonde, qui vont toucher plus ou moins bas le fond du même océan— la durée pure.[23]

22. *Cloître,* p. 310.
23. *Péguy,* 1, 38.

Rolland used almost the same words to describe his "histoire des âmes." In his *Péguy,* however, he defends the originality of his historical vision against the possibility of Bergsonian influence. Bergson might indeed have been one of his metaphysical "éclairs," but Rolland arrived at the same conclusions independently—intuitively —some fifteen years before publication of the *Introduction à la métaphysique.* In his re-creation of the period of his association with Péguy, Rolland underlines the seven years' difference in age between himself and his associate, which for Rolland placed them in separate intellectual generations and set him (Rolland) apart from the group of Bergson's disciples: "Voilà pourquoi je ne fus point de ceux qui faisaient cénacle, aux vendredis du Collège de France; il me suffisait de savoir que sa parole ajoutait une confirmation illuminée à l'enfant Christophe qui était venu me visiter." [24]

The hero of *Jean-Christophe* is immersed in the ocean of being from the beginning of his existence in *L'Aube.* It is as if Rolland wished to baptize his creature, to put him under the sign of the intuition of the universe which he himself had received while reading Spinoza, before involving Christophe in the linear development of the fictional hero. Christophe shares Rolland's intuition from the cradle; it is this which distinguishes him from the "unheroic" characters around him. The first sentence of the book invokes the patronage of the river even before it places the newborn protagonist on the scene: "Le grondement du fleuve monte derrière la maison." [25] The images of the first pages, the first chapters, of the book are all water, as if to create a reservoir from which the entire history can draw: the river roars behind the house, rain falls, moisture condenses on the panes of the windows of Christophe's house, and the infant partakes instinctively in this flow by imbibing his mother's milk and by his tears, with their suggestion of the pain inherent in the intuition of life. The passage of these first days is an ebb and flow of the ocean's tide, infinite in substance and indivisible, given identity only by its movement (reflected, as is fre-

24. Ibid., p. 39.
25. *Jean-Christophe,* p. 3. All subsequent citations of the novel will be found in parentheses in the text.

quently the case in Rolland's lyric passages, by alexandrine prose patterns):

> Le vaste flot des jours se déroule lentement. Immuables, le jour et la nuit remontent et redescendent, comme le flux et le reflux d'une mer infinie. Les semaines et les mois s'écoulent et recommencent. Et la suite des jours est comme un même jour. (p. 11)

This, of course, is the "given" for any human being launched at birth on the limitless sea of existence. But Christophe, the hero and creator, is distinguished from the usual literary hero by his intuition from birth of the nature of things and by his possession of an answering flood of life-force within him, which partakes of the external flow (if anything can be called external in the omnipresent, penetrating force of existence). His soul reproduces this flow in miniature, but it cries out in rage and defiance at its imprisonment in the feeble body of a child; Christophe dimly senses "l'océan bouillonnant qui gronde dans l'étroite prison de ce petit corps d'enfant . . . . Son être est sans limites. Il est tout ce qui est" (p. 11). Within this unformed being is the germ of the law which dictates all he will become. Nothing is absent, because the individual existence, as nature *naturée* and *naturante* at the same time, received from its inception all of the qualities it will create for itself in the duration of its temporal existence.

Rolland gives the young Christophe his first conscious intuition of the nature of things, of the course of his life and its law, in a scene of *L'Aube* which remained one of the author's predilections in the whole roman-fleuve. The boy, having renounced music in defiance of his father's ambitions for him and been beaten for it, contemplates the Rhine from the hall window of his house (pp. 64–70). Many of the elements of the author's own revelation of Spinoza are present in the scene. The unhappy child, forced into an exploitation of his talent against his will, imprisoned with only a narrow window opening out onto a larger horizon (whose vastness and importance is magnified by this frame-like restriction of his perceptions), suddenly feels liberated by an intuition of the reality

of his existence: Rolland through the impact of the words before
him, which seem to open his soul out into the world, and Christophe
through the spectacle of the river, "un être,—inexplicable, mais
combien plus puissant que tous ceux qu'il connaissait!" (p. 67).
The movement of the stream carries Christophe's spirit along with
it, and in this motion the boy visualizes charming and mysterious
figures, eternally present in the substance of time, but out of the
future of his own life-stream:

> Quelles sont ces images qui pénètrent l'enfant d'un trouble
> passionné? Jamais il ne les avait vues; et pourtant il les con-
> naissait: il les a reconnues. D'où viennent-elles? De quel gouffre
> obscur de l'Etre? Est-ce de ce qui fut . . . *ou de ce qui sera?*
> (p. 69)

The movement of the stream carries him past the monuments of his
life to be, past the ephemeral witnesses of this enduring reality flowing within him, until it widens out into the motionless, indivisible,
and endless expanse of the sea:

> Le fleuve court à elle. Elle semble courir à lui. Elle l'aspire. Il
> la veut. Il va disparaître . . . . L'âme libre fend l'espace, comme
> le vol des hirondelles ivres d'air, qui traversent le ciel avec des
> cris aigus . . . . Joie! Joie! Il n'y a plus rien! . . . O bonheur
> infini! (p. 69)

It is out of this intuition of the nature of the universe and of his
life's relation to it that Christophe has his first related intuition of
the nature of music. The entire scene is accompanied by a variety of
music of the spheres, or rather music of the earth and water, which
is the stuff of his inspiration. It negates the child's determination to
turn away from his art and the temptation of death. This pattern
will continue throughout his life: Christophe emerges for a time
into the world of events, loses his intimate relation with this inner
stream and its external correspondence, but always returns to the
rhythmic flood of life-force for his inspiration, for his sense of reality
and necessity in a chaotic universe.

In spite of the exclamations and the rhetorical questions to which

Rolland was prone in his lyric style, this passage is a powerfully effective moment in the architecture of the novel. Several important psychological themes have already been introduced. Christophe has had his first revelations of music, which is now associated for him with both pleasure and pain: music is identified with profound emotional reactions in the unformed consciousness of the child, as well as with fantasies which represent his nearest approach thus far to internal vision, but the first appearance of his musical talent has encouraged his father to exploit him and to force him to practice long hours against his will. The conflict between vision and virtuosity, the internal world and worldly success, is thus already posited.

The association of pain with music and of music with internal vision is instrumental to the transformation of the ocean image into that of the river, which takes place here organically for the first time. Christophe's experience is like that of Rolland contemplating the Rhine for the first time, effectively, in 1896. In both circumstances, the formulation of a dominant motive image takes place. However, the levels of experience are quite different in the two cases. Rolland's experience gave a nominal identity to an image which had already certainly undergone organic transformation. Christophe's is the elementary transformation in the process of occurring. Direction is being given to formlessness; the image of immanence and all-being becomes the flow of individuated life-force across time toward its ultimate identity with the ocean at death.

For the first time as well, the structure of the novel is openly identified with the river image and, by extension, with the concept of musical structure that the latter conveys. One is reminded of Rolland's letter to Malwida, of the organic growth, triumph, and fall of a dominant emotive theme. Christophe's emotional "given," represented by the ocean and the permeating waters of his infancy at the beginning of *L'Aube,* is here channeled into event, especially the promise of future event growing out of his current state. Similarly, point of view in the novel is clearly represented by the river's current as the element of consciousness and movement and the fixed landmarks of the shore as passing external events and exterior characters, to be viewed from the river and to disappear as each successive stage of the hero's life is passed.

If Christophe's consciousness can be described as a moving point in the current's flow, the eternally renewed stream of the rest of the river becomes memory—and, by natural extension of the image, memory includes those areas of the river's flow which *precede* the hero's consciousness as well. That is indeed what happens in this passage. It is evident from this to what extent Rolland's thinking was molded by the image, by the creative power of the musical motive which formulates psychology, event, and structure in his novel.

Renan: "la route en lacets"

This metaphorical "substance" of the law governing the hero and the creative artist, evolved from Rolland's personal adaptation of Spinoza's concepts, does not give more than a general idea of its workings and importance. It was the foundation of a more elaborate pattern of principles inspired by some of the other writers under whose influence Rolland came during his formative years. It is necessary to examine the action of other metaphorical motives he drew from the ideas of Renan, Goethe, and Tolstoy, which gave shape and direction to Spinoza's life-force in his idea of the history of art and then in the life of his hero and the architecture of the novel.

During the years in which Rolland's original conception of the novel was maturing, his metaphorical vision of the life-current was being shaped by professional and personal experiences: his stable, even static image of life was put to test by conflicting pressures which tended to disturb the premature serenity the young author had attempted to achieve by his metaphysical credo. Evidences of Rolland's desire to reconcile conflicting tendencies, to harmonize dissonant forces and attractions in his intellectual life, can be seen as early as the *Credo quia verum*. The principal vectors there— Spinoza, Renan, "Renaissance passion," Tolstoy—were not startlingly different from the ones which acted upon him later. Even the major poles of attraction, the "Dream" and "Action," between which he felt torn, are part of his attempt to reconcile opposites. Rolland, however, had not yet understood the active principle which was to be involved in his novelistic formulation of the hero's internal law. Although his symbolic representation of the life-stream involved both human time (the life of the individual, the sequence of generations in history) and eternity, in which these units of time were generated and contained, he had not yet realized the internal nature of human time and its contact with chronological time through event. What was missing from the structure of his life-metaphor was the concept of becoming, in both the historical and individual sense.

Rolland's experiences following his departure from the Ecole Normale helped him to penetrate this interaction between internal life and event through time. His opportunities to confront ideal and principle with action contributed greatly to this: for example, the conflict between the contemplative and active aspects of his career as scholar and teacher. A more striking case is the moral stalemate created in his life by conflicting principles and allegiances in the Dreyfus affair. Rolland, it can be felt from his later comments, learned a powerful lesson from his incapacity to decide between the opposing sides of the case. On the one hand, he was tied by family bonds and a strong sense of attachment to the soil of France to the anti-Dreyfus side; on the other, his relation through marriage to a Jewish milieu, active on the opposing side, and his strong sense of justice drew him toward the pro-Dreyfus faction.[26] His political sympathies, republican turning socialist, and his general disdain for the military should have been deciding factors, yet the conflict of principles and a passionate desire not to compromise any of them led him to inaction.

Rolland never completely rid himself of this tendency to weigh conflicting forces against each other, to strive for a balance. However, his dissatisfaction with the attempt to hold them in static equilibrium, as he did in the Dreyfus affair, must have been a contributing factor in the emergence of a pattern of alternation through time that characterizes his thought from this period. One symptom of this pattern is his new understanding of the personality of Goethe, whom he begins to see as an embodiment of the process of

26. This is the moral problem dramatized in Rolland's play from the same period, *Les Loups,* which evoked violent reactions on both sides of the political fence.

harmonization acting through time. But the pattern of alternation, of dialectic movement and synthesis, which begins to shape Rolland's thinking can be traced to ideas suggested to him by readings in Renan and by an interview he had with the aging writer in 1886.

Renan's influence on Rolland's thinking becomes apparent in his diary of the Ecole Normale, in which he noted the action of the author of *Le Prêtre de Nemi* upon his intellectual life. After reading that work, which made a strong impression on him, he bought *L'Abbesse de Jouarre* as soon as it was published. Among his entries from the beginning of his stay at the school is Rolland's résumé of the latter work's "message": "Tout ce qui est, doit être. Ce qui est réel, est bon. Ce qui est plus réel est meilleur. Ce qui triomphe est plus réel, donc meilleur. Ne soyons donc pas inquiets de l'avenir. Tout ce qui est sert à ce qui sera, au Devenir infini." [27]

In a letter to Renan written two months later (December 21, 1886), Rolland submitted this résumé, slightly elaborated, for the author's criticism. He added the comment that he alone, among the students at the Ecole Normale, considered Renan a stoic, a judgment which the others viewed as paradoxical. He admitted that he could not entirely share Renan's ideas, but he nevertheless found them to possess an inspiring "elevation." He said of this philosophy, as he understood it, "Je vois peu de doctrines plus nobles, plus sereines que celle de vos deux derniers drames." [28]

Renan surprised Rolland by replying immediately to his letter, complimenting him on his acuity, and inviting him to a visit at the Collège de France to discuss "a few shadings" of the ideas suggested in the letter. Armed with youthful courage, Rolland accepted the invitation the following Sunday. The great man talked charmingly and graciously with him for an hour or more on a variety of subjects, including modern Russian literature, the future of humanity, and the role of religion and philosophy in the progress of mankind. Rolland's reaction to Renan's cultivated objectivity was mixed; over the years, looking back on the episode, he tended to view Renan more and more critically, as his retrospective commentary

27. *Cloître*, p. 7.
28. Ibid., p. 20.

on this interview, written in 1912 and published in *Le Cloître de la rue d'Ulm,* indicates. Renan's unconcern for the doubt and despair of the modern Everyman, "liberated" from the comforts of religion by the progress of science, and his "heartless little laugh" increasingly dominated Rolland's impressions of their conversation. Yet he eliminated this consideration from the version of the episode published fifty years later in *Compagnons de route,* as if, in the long run, he acknowledged a debt to the philosopher which he had unjustly denied in the interim. He now judged Renan's influence upon him in accordance with the place he assigned to Renan in intellectual history:

> Riche musique d'une époque de transition, chargée de passé, abondante en avenir, pour qui le temps n'est pas venu encore de faire l'unité dans sa pensée mouvante; mais qui, à cette heure ultime de gestation quiète, savoure les jeux et les combats de son intelligence aux multiples accords.[29]

With Renan, as with Spinoza, it seems to have been not a philosophical system which influenced Rolland, but the impact of a few phrases and the echo which they awakened in him. He rejected from the beginning Renan's ironic attitude toward human history, the "comfortably superhuman, cozily inhuman dreams, in his *Philosophical Dialogues,*"[30] but Renanian phrases keep recurring in Rolland's works as leit-motivs. It seems certain that they had great importance in the workings of a mind which always tended to synthesize its attitudes around such fixed linguistic and image patterns.

First of all, and most pervasive, is the obsession with the idea of Becoming which Rolland inherited from Renan. Renan's personal idea of the nature of human progress, expressed in the interview, seems to have remained in Rolland's mind, and not the more prevalent scientistic optimism of the times—that is to say, the concept of *devenir,* which does not envision a final static perfection, but in which the movement of Becoming itself is the end and in which the final victory is the sum of all the process of evolution which has gone

29. *Compagnons de route,* p. 148.
30. *Péguy,* 1, 82.

before. Renan replied to Rolland's question of whether human perfection was a thing of the foreseeable future by saying that our planet would still be in existence in 100,000 years. It was inconceivable to Renan that man's development would not continue to fill that space. Meanwhile, men would continue to be imperfect, following their irregular but definite path of spiritual and physical evolution.[31]

Rolland's adaptations of this thought are multiform in his view of the history of art and of the life of the individual artist and hero. In the days of his youthful pessimism (for Rolland became more sanguine about the future of mankind as he advanced in years), he tended to consider this perpetual evolution of men's thoughts and perceptions, artistic and otherwise, as destructive, a dissolution of the universal *one* in complexity:

> Rien, mieux que la musique ne me fait voir ce que je suis et ce que nous serons, l'avenir et la mort de notre humanité. Nous marchons vers le quart de ton. Un temps viendra où Beethoven paraîtra fade et monotone à ceux qui auront creusé plus avant dans le champ de la sensation auditive. D'une façon générale, nos sensations tendent à se décomposer.[32]

If this movement from original unity toward multiplicity might be defined by some as "progress," it seemed to promise the death of what Rolland held most dear. It implied the impermanence and decomposition of artistic creation and therefore rendered it meaningless. Later, however, under the influence of Tolstoy's less metaphysical idea of the role and nature of art, Rolland became reconciled to the justice of this progression and the engulfment of past greatness in the stream of time. He came to see in this process not the destruction of what had been, but the continual, necessary renewal of the artistic experience, which would otherwise become stagnant. This attitude is especially evident in the most Tolstoyan of his writings, *Le Théâtre du peuple,* which appeared in the *Cahiers de la Quinzaine* in November of 1903. There he proclaims not only the

31. *Cloître,* p. 24.

32. *Cloître,* p. 44. The influence of his recent studies in pre-Socratic philosophy is evident here.

internal necessity of the renewal of artistic expression but, conversely, the harmfulness of clinging to outmoded art forms: "Un art passé ne suffit jamais à la vie; et souvent il risque de lui nuire. La condition nécessaire d'une vie saine et normale, c'est la production d'un art incessamment renouvelé, au fur et à mesure de la vie." [33] If he describes as direct experience the aesthetic and emotional impact of a performance of a work as old and outmoded as Monteverdi's *Orfeo* (in a letter of 1906), it is only because of his intuition of its freshness and its relevance to the time in which it was created:

> Il n'y a rien de plus beau au monde. Il n'y a rien de pareil. Tous ceux qui l'entendent en sont saisis. Songez à ce que peut donner un génie dans un genre tout neuf, avec une langue musicale toute fraîche, sur laquelle ne pèse aucune formule, aucun ressouvenir.[34]

This was an intuition open only to the "initié," however, to the members of the minority of which Rolland was a part by background and education, if not by will. In striking contrast is his contemporary statement concerning Wagner's *Tristan,* which he had once felt was the most enduring of the master's works because of its classic purity.

> Mais, tandis que l'autre soir je l'écoutais, je pensais malgré moi: 'Tu passeras, toi; tu iras rejoindre Gluck, Bach, Monteverdi, Palestrina, toutes les grandes âmes dont le nom persiste parmi les hommes, mais dont les hommes ne sentent plus les pensées, sauf une poignée d'initiés qui s'efforcent en vain de ressusciter le passé. . . . Le monde continue sa marche, avide de nouvelles émotions, et son Désir incessamment monte et se brise.' [35]

This conflict between past glory and present life in art is the basis of Rolland's violent criticism in *La Révolte* of musical life in Germany. Christophe castigates the aesthetes of his provincial city for their idolization of German masters of the past and their judgment

33. *Théâtre du peuple,* p. 14.
34. *Chère Sofia, I,* 253.
35. *Musiciens d'aujourd'hui,* pp. 82–83.

of contemporary music by their measure. If the classics must be worshipped at the expense of the continued development of musical creation, then Christophe would rather see them destroyed. He remains true to this evaluation of the importance of the great artists of the past to the moment when, on his deathbed, he has a revelation of the nature of art:

> Plus vite que toute autre, la langue musicale se brûle; au bout d'un siècle ou deux, elle n'est plus comprise que de quelques initiés. Pour qui existent encore Monteverdi et Lully? Déjà, la mousse ronge les chênes de la forêt classique. Nos constructions sonores, où chantent nos passions, seront des temples vides, s'écrouleront dans l'oubli. (p. 1587)

Christophe, however, does not apply this law of change merely to the progression of styles in music through history. Even stronger than his revolt against the petrifaction of past creative life in classicism is his reaction against a similar force in himself. From the beginning, he is conscious of the moral and functional necessity of his artistic Becoming if he is to participate in the life-force which imbues all creativity. At first, as in *Le Matin,* where the composer is just dimly conscious of the forces within and around him, the knowledge comes in ephemeral intuitions akin to Roquentin's in *La Nausée,* only less general, more self-directed—a disgust, not with all of being, but with the grotesquely confused image of stability in the moment, survival of the past, and foreshadowings of the future which Christophe sees in his mirror:

> S'il se voit dans son miroir, il ne se reconnaît pas. Cette face large et rouge, ces sourcils proéminents, ces petits yeux enfoncés, ce nez court, gros du bout, aux narines dilatées, cette lourde mâchoire, cette bouche boudeuse, tout ce masque, laid et vulgaire, lui est étranger. (p. 146)

Even more strongly, the creative artist reflected in his past works seems foreign, disgusting, and meaningless to him. "Il ne se reconnaît pas davantage dans ses oeuvres. Il se juge, il sait la nullité de ce qu'il fait, de ce qu'il est" (p. 146). It is not stability, the apprehension of landmarks in the unceasing movement of his life, which gives consolation to the young genius-to-be. It is the certitude he has of the continuity of his Becoming, his development in the future—even though, at this point, Rolland makes it clear that the child Christophe has not yet arrived at a full awareness of the process. In his vague trust in this future, Christophe visualizes his fulfillment as an arrival at the *status* of greatness, at a stasis in which the promise of the present will take concrete and immutable shape:

> Quoi qu'il fasse, quoi qu'il pense, aucune de ses pensées, de ses actions, de ses oeuvres, ne l'enferme ni ne l'exprime; il le sait, il a ce sentiment étrange, que ce qu'il est le plus, ce n'est pas ce qu'il est à présent, c'est ce qu'il *sera demain . . . . Il sera!* (pp. 146–47)

As Christophe becomes more aware of the nature of Becoming, he loses the illusion of future stability, concentrating on the continuation of the life-process without reference to any goal. He gives up the thought of interrupting his development long enough to allow the public to catch up to him. The concept of Becoming postulates that the creator must be a prophet. There is a breathless inexorability in Christophe's progress toward his future, which causes an incurable malaise in those around him, friends and enemies, and which heightens the solitude his genius brings upon him. But music is also the consolation for the restless loneliness of Becoming. This can be seen in the beginning of the last volume of *Jean-Christophe* where, under the epigraph of Schubert's *An die Musik,* Rolland writes:

> La vie passe. Le corps et l'âme s'écoulent comme un flot. Les ans s'inscrivent sur la chair de l'arbre qui vieillit. Le monde entier des formes s'use et se renouvelle. Toi seule ne passes pas, immortelle Musique. Tu es la mer intérieure. Tu es l'âme profonde. (p. 1431)

Having arrived at a final comprehension of the unceasing necessity of his Becoming, Christophe realizes that the process must continue within himself until death, when his individuality is engulfed by the immobile sea which contains the totality of movement in time and space. In the ultimate apotheosis of Saint Christopher, the bearer of Christ, the composer, arriving at the endpoint of his individual Becoming, rejoins the stream of embodiments of this law of the historical past; his sequence of movement becomes a point in the larger sequence of time which composes the Unity in its eternal progression. Like his predecessors—Bach, Handel, Gluck, Beethoven, Wagner—Christophe has reached the limit of development which his law of Becoming and the place allotted to him in the total stream of development permit. In a sense his life is a pre-destined failure: like the great artists who have gone before him, he could never hope to attain the culminating point of the stream of Becoming. But here Rolland rejoins the sanguine pessimism of Renan's *Prêtre de Nemi:* "Antistius renaîtra éternellement pour échouer éternellement, et, en définitive, il se trouvera que la totalité de ses échecs vaudra une victoire." [36]

Inherent in this process of Becoming, as defined by Renan, is a particular form of movement. In his conversation with Rolland in 1886 he illustrated it by an image which became one of the patterns of Rolland's historical and artistic thought. During Rolland's later self-imposed exile from France, he entitled an article *La route en lacets qui monte,*[37] recalling the words which Renan had used thirty years before: "Le chemin de l'humanité est une route de montagne: elle monte en lacets; elle a des coudes, des détours; on dirait, par moments, qu'on tourne le dos au but. Main on s'en rapproche toujours." [38] For Renan this expressed the philosopher's detached view of the march of humanity throughout its history, the intellectual's consolation for the fact that his theory of human progress is difficult, if not impossible, to substantiate by reference to the events of his lifetime. One senses the condescension with which the old man threw out these scraps of comfort to an adolescent who needed them to retain hope in the ideal of progress. Rolland was struck by the ironic laugh with which Renan described the tortuous route that

36. Renan, *Oeuvres complètes d' Ernest Renan* (35 vols. Paris, Calmann Lévy, 1863–1926), 27, 261.
37. Published in *Les Précurseurs* (Paris, 1919).
38. *Compagnons de route,* pp. 144–45.

humanity had to follow in its struggle toward the heights. The final words of the philosopher, near the end of his life, to the young man ready to embark on his, were: "La vie est excellente; mais ce n'est pas grand'chose . . . . Le vrai philosophe est brave; il se fait mieux tuer que les autres. Il voit la vanité de tout." [39]

The form of Renan's image of progress, if not his personal attitude, was integrated into Rolland's idea of music history and the spiritual progress of his musician. Rolland gave the "route en lacets qui monte" a peculiar shape, one which was characteristic of this art more than any other. He outlines this point of view most clearly in the article "De la place de la musique dans l'histoire générale," referred to above. Tracing the graph of progress in Western history from the Greeks to the present, with the exchange of political and intellectual leadership among different nations of Europe, Rolland sees a relationship between the fortunes of government and the musical expression emanating from them, which was not a parallelism but a counterpoint. Music seems frequently to be strangely out of phase with the political spirit of a time, to contradict the idea of art which one expects an era to produce. During the decadence of Rome, when everything else was in chaos and turmoil, the "abominable Caesars" and their barbaric successors alike were "mad for concerts." From this period of disintegration arose the foundations of "an art as perfect, as pure, as the most accomplished creations of happy eras," [40] the Gregorian chant, whose masterpieces date from the invasions of the Goths and the Lombards. Tracing the graph further, through the Carolingians and their decline, he finds a "happy flowering of music, in spite of everything, enduring through the social upheavals" and concludes: "Ainsi, la musique nous montre ici la continuité de la vie sous la mort apparente, l'éternel renouveau sous la ruine du monde." [41] In his thesis concerning the place of music in the study of history, this art completes the image which one can gain of an era, an image which could only be imperfect without the frequently contrary testimony musical creation gives.

39. Ibid., p. 148.
40. *Musiciens d'autrefois*, p. 6.
41. Ibid., p. 7.

Thus, in a sense, Rolland extends the idea of man's progress on a zigzag path to emphasize the importance in music of the "turns backward," the periods of retrogression in the uneven ascent of civilization. He does not deny that all stages of man's development have produced their music, and he qualifies this apparent dependence of musical progress on social and political destruction to the extent of identifying the flourishing of "social" music, music of a public nature, with periods of advancement. The more internal music, however, which penetrates deeply into the timeless area within, finds its fruition in those periods which tend to isolate men, to drive them into communion with their inner nature. Although Rolland felt the continual conflict for dominance of these ideas of music within himself, his profoundest, if involuntary sympathy went toward the latter.

Rolland did not restrict his application of this law to the history of music in the distant past. Writing in 1904 for a German public, in Richard Strauss' series *Die Musik,* Rolland traces the renascence of French musical life through the previous thirty-five years, basing his analysis on the premise that "Les désastres de la guerre de 1870 régénérèrent l'esprit artistique de la nation. La musique en sentit les effets immédiats." [42] His study examines this development in terms of the spread of musical education, the flourishing of concerts in Paris and elsewhere, the return to popular sources for inspiration, and an immense increase in the production of excellent new music, at first under the influence of Wagner's reforms, and later in reaction to them. Citing the deplorable state of French music before France's defeat by the Prussians—"Combien de gens ont jugé, d'après cette période, qu'il en avait toujours été ainsi, et que la France n'était pas un peuple musical!"—Rolland states that the role played by music in this period of political and cultural brilliance is epitomized by Hugo's alleged statement about Germany: that Germany's inferiority "can be measured by her musical superiority." [43] Rolland expresses the fear that the success which music was experiencing in his time might destroy the sources of its re-

42. "Le Renouveau," in *Musiciens d'aujourd'hui,* p. 215.
43. Ibid., p. 213. Cf. also Gobineau's views on the racial inferiority of the musically gifted African Negroes.

vival: the spiritual withdrawal into deeper areas of the stream of French artistic experience. France's musical health depended, in his view, on constant renewal following the law of Becoming. Success threatened it with stagnancy born out of exaggerated veneration of the formulas of present greatness.[44]

As evidence of the converse of this rule, Rolland elsewhere cites the degeneration of German music following Wagner's death and the Prussian military victory over France. Swept along by political expansion and the facile success of their works, German artists were unable to withdraw into themselves and undergo the necessary period of reconcentration of their artistic sensibilities and powers. In both these instances Rolland sees the workings of a law of irregular movement, which he derived from Renan.

Rolland does not apply this movement merely to the historical progress of music. It is found in his works in more individual terms, as the law of the life of the creative man. Renan gave the example in the works by which Rolland was influenced—the philosophical dramas. One of their salient ideas is an application of the law of irregular progression to the individual characters who promote human progress. The moral development of Renan's protagonists, who represent stages in the route of mankind toward perfection, is calculated on this pattern, which dismisses the possibility of a linear human progress. Historical movement requires the alternation of forward and backward motion, of the "good" and the "bad"; the distinction between the irregular and the linear is the same as that between the "real" and the "ideal." This irregular process is expressed in the moral life of the individual by the conflict between doubt and certainty, vice and virtue, passion and reason, the latter pair being elemental to the philosophical tendencies of these dramas.

In Renan's *Caliban,* a sequel to Shakespeare's *Tempest,* this principle is embodied in the choice of Caliban, "a formless being, scarcely rough-sketched, on its way to becoming a man," as the spiritual heir of Prospero in the forward movement of mankind—not Ariel, "his aerial agent." The conflicting presence of good and evil is necessary for movement to take place. Perfection is a stasis. Both perfection

44. Ibid., p. 277.

and the opposing imperfection must be embraced by the sage, or he risks becoming lost in abstraction:

> Au fond, l'éternelle raison se fait jour par les moyens les plus opposés en apparence. . . . 'J'ai aimé la justice et j'ai haï l'iniquité,' disait un grand pape. On peut toujours aimer la justice; mais haïr l'iniquité! . . . C'est plus facile à dire qu'à faire.[45]

This attitude is even more explicit in the sequel, *L'Eau de Jouvence.* Caliban's initial baseness and ingratitude are seen there as essential to the movement of progress. The character himself sees them as the basis of his superiority over Ariel, whom he chides for his perfection: "Petit fat, qui ne peux te rendre compte de ce qu'il y a de mérite pour l'homme sorti du limon à secouer la lourde croûte terreuse et à forcer la herse dont s'entourent les hommes à la peau blanche et au sang vermeil." [46] Prospero, near the moment of his death, finds that "the cup of life is delicious," not despite, but because of, the inequalities and contradictions which it contains. He elaborates the idea into a law of universal and individual movement based on the apparently conflicting forces of life: "Sans Caliban, point d'histoire. Les grognements de Caliban, l'âpre haine qui le porte à supplanter son maître, sont le principe du mouvement dans l'humanité . . . . Le monde est un cercle immense où la pourriture sort de la vie et la vie de la pourriture." [47]

In *Le Prêtre de Nemi,* which Rolland considered at the time of his conversation with Renan to be the most significant of the *drames philosophiques,* Renan applies this law of development to his protagonist more directly. Antistius' chief fault is his achievement of a perfection beyond the reach of his age. His intuition of the divinity he serves, of the superior morality toward which imperfect mankind is moving, separates him from the masses whom he desires to influence and predestines him for a futile martyrdom. His beliefs, which are the detached philosophical ideals of Renan him-

45. *Oeuvres complètes, 27,* 99–100.
46. Ibid., pp. 242–43.
47. Ibid., p. 244.

self, will of course be vindicated by the eventual pattern of intellectual progress. But it is not enough to be right. It is necessary to be relevant to one's time. Antistius himself takes increasing account of that fact up to the time of his death at the hands of his bandit-successor, and Renan suggests that it is this loss of certainty in perfection which finally constitutes Antistius' real moral superiority. The comprehension of the ultimate end is incomplete without experiencing the imperfect and conflicting stages which lead up to it. In terms of individual morality, "Nous n'estimons . . . la haute moralité que si elle a traversé le doute; nous ne voulons nous décider pour le bien qu'après nous être faits contre lui les avocats du mal." [48]

In the same way the Abbesse de Jouarre gains moral stature as a result of her "fall." Her step backward in succumbing to a lover sets in motion the reaction which carries her further in her moral development than she could have gone without this fall from grace. Renan's desire to escape from metaphysical ideals to a human- and life-oriented philosophy led him to embrace the irregular and imperfect as more in accordance with reality, more consequent with human progress and greatness. The "route en lacets qui monte" was as pertinent to individual moral growth as to the all-embracing perspective of human history.

Renan's suggestion of the winding mountain road as a metaphor of human progress took root in Rolland's mind, to a great extent because of the latter's long-standing love of Alpine landscapes. This was a taste which the author never lost and which took precedence in his sentiments over the marine vista, despite the importance of the ocean for him as a symbol. Rolland was moved by his direct experiences of the sea (viewed from the shore), as some of his earliest memories testify.[49] A note from his diary in 1907 indicates how powerful its effect was on him: "Toute la nuit, la grandiose musique de l'océan qui monte: le rythme de son souffle puissant, et, sous ces grands accords, le frémissement sans fin des flots, comme le vent dans une forêt." [50] But the experience of the sea was not essentially

48. Ibid., p. 260.
49. See *Voyage intérieur*, pp. 24–27.
50. "Voyage en Espagne," in *Europe*, No. 109–10 (Jan.–Feb. 1955), p. 74.

agreeable for Rolland. It tended to fatigue and enervate him, whereas the mountains exerted a tonic effect: "Je n'y puis rester, elle me fatigue, elle m'énerve, elle m'empêche de dormir, et je finis par avoir l'oppression fiévreuse de son perpétuel: 'Ahan!', surtout la nuit."[51]

It is not surprising that Rolland attempted to reconcile and synthesize in his literary work these apparently contradictory forces, "the mountains and the sea, those convulsive forces,"[52] which exerted such a different fascination. An early indication of the attempt can be found in the Ecole Normale diary, in a project for a musical drama, "a mystical fairy tale," to be written with Suarès. The three parts of the work, entitled "La Montagne," "La Mer," and "La Cathédrale," were to represent respectively "egotistical, passionate action," "passionate love," and a final renunciation of these in "the mystical possession of the divine."[53] If the mountain and the sea represent contrasting phases of the hero's struggle, they are still linked and synthesized in Rolland's mind: the identity of this synthesis with the image of the cathedral is an interesting foreshadowing of *Dans la Maison* and *La Nouvelle Journée*.

The opposition between sea and mountain was not so absolute in Rolland's mind as one might expect. There are signs of his desire to explain the apparent paradox, during the same period, in another passage of the *Cloître de la rue d'Ulm*:

> On attribue le mouvement à la mer, par opposition à la montagne immobile. Erreur: il y a plus de mouvement dans la montagne. D'une part, l'élan de bas en haut,—une aspiration plus puissante que celle des cathédrales gothiques. De l'autre, la chute dans l'abîme, vertige, disparition, mort.[54]

Again the connection with the cathedral appears, but here there is a stronger tendency to mingle and exchange the traditional connotations of the two dominant symbols, to arrive at a synthesis with-

51. Letter to Sofia Bertolini, June 1908, in *Chère Sofia, 1,* 346.
52. *De Jean-Christophe à Colas Breugnon,* p. 164.
53. *Cloître,* p. 264: it is interesting to note that Rolland intended to write "La Montagne" himself, leaving "La Mer" to Suarès and collaborating with him on "La Cathédrale."
54. Ibid., p. 251.

in the context of one or the other, which culminates for the moment in an attribution of the sea's qualities to the mountain: "Mais la montagne a cet élément vivant: le nuage, l'air liquide, et toute la série de ses métamorphoses, le torrent, la cascade, la couleur changeante." [55]

By the time of *Jean-Christophe,* however, with the evolution of the ocean metaphor into the dominant symbol of the river, Rolland tends to direct his synthesis more toward the liquid context. For one thing, the river already represents the influence of this pattern of change through time, if not the quality of alternation or reversal. For another, the river is too central to the conception of the novel to be displaced, except momentarily, by the mountain road. Yet the latter, only imperfectly absorbed by the liquid metaphor, emerges from time to time in important places when Rolland has need of an image giving a more powerful sense of transcendent motion than that of the river joining the sea. A striking example of this, as we shall see, occurs near the end of the novel, in *La Nouvelle Journée.*

In his application of the mountain road pattern to the spiritual and artistic development of his hero, Rolland involves him, from the first volumes of *Jean-Christophe,* in a series of rises and falls, which only by variations of context and situation avoid excessive regularity. At times the pattern is expressed in terms of Christophe's aesthetic and artistic growth; at other times in terms of his religious and moral experience, his emotional life—friendship and love—or his physical and social condition. On the surface, there does not seem to be any specific rhythm to this pattern. It almost seems that Rolland's faithfulness to this particular law of creative life was instinctive rather than explicitly applied from without, yet he acknowledged his consciousness of it in a letter to Sofia Bertolini in March 1905:

> Certains très braves gens, protestants de race ou de coeur . . . ont été un peu désorientés, choqués, blessés par le 3ᵉ [book of *Jean-Christophe*]. Ainsi Gabriel Monod . . . . Il imaginait un développement de Christophe, en ligne droite toujours, toujours pur, et conscient de son but. . . . Le vie n'est pas si simple

55. Ibid.

qu'ils pensent; et ce n'est pas une oeuvre de volonté. Moins que toutes,—les grandes vies.[56]

Its influence becomes obvious to the reader, who comes to expect these fluctuations as an integral part of the hero's character, internally and in his relationship with the world. These fluctuations are, however, especially evident in the volumes of the book having most to do with the internal development of Christophe and far less in *La Foire sur la Place* and *Dans la Maison,* where, for the most part, the hero ceases to exist in and for himself and becomes a subjective eye for the author's critical observation of the artistic milieus of Paris.

The mountain road manifests itself in *Jean-Christophe* in two principal manners: as pattern and as image, more frequently the former. Since it is less basic, or less central, to Rolland's thought (as modality rather than substance), its workings are less insistently and continually apparent. It tends to be closely accompanied, whether through chance or design, by an appearance of the river image, as if to underline the fact that it is really a function of the latter.

The operation of the pattern bearing the closest analogy with its Renanian model is in Jean-Christophe's religious evolution. The importance of this aspect of the hero's life should not be underestimated: it is pertinent, even essential, not only to his character per se but to the idea of artistic genius which Rolland meant to embody in him. Christophe's creativity is a constant dialogue, at times in unison, at times in revolt, with the Creator. If, at the end of the novel, the hero achieves a final reconciliation with the Almighty— the assumption of Saint Christopher into the bosom of God—alternate, conflicting stages leading up to it are no less significant than the final resolution. The falls from grace are part of the ultimate state of grace itself, as in Renan's idea of human progress.

In the books relating Christophe's youth, this pattern bears a marked resemblance to the life of the author. Rolland has recounted the oscillations of his faith, beginning with the contradictory influences of his parents. His father, a freethinker, nevertheless held

56. *Chère Sofia,* 1, 216.

that religion was "good for children"; [57] but the faith of his mother tended to have a counterbalancing influence. Rolland describes himself during this period as searching for the faith which he respected but did not sincerely feel, unwilling to penetrate too deeply into the recesses of his soul for fear of discovering the truth, until he was transported from the stability of Clamecy into the "atmosphère déicide" of Paris in the 1880s at the age of fifteen. There his inevitable loss of faith, or rather his acknowledgment of its loss, took place. Rolland emphasizes not only the psychological seriousness of this acknowledgment but the essentially religious nature of his renunciation, which takes on the character of an affirmation rather than a negation:

> Mon premier acte d'énergie, à cette heure d'adolescence où je sombrais sans Dieu, fut de rompre avec ma religion.—Ce fut mon acte le plus religieux. . . . Par respect pour moi-même et pour le Dieu caché, je n'ai pas voulu feindre, mimer le semblant de croire, recrépir la façade, m'obstiner à pratiquer." [58]

Of course the search continued in the hope of finding at least a substitute for orthodoxy. It culminated for the moment in the "éclair de Spinoza" and in the mystical experience of universal love which overwhelmed him on the Janicular Hill, "tel Saül l'antichrist".[59]

The hero of the novel passes through a similar series of crises under similar influences. His first vague experiences of the divinity are connected with music. The bells of Saint-Martin's, heard in his cradle (Rolland's childhood memories are present here, even in the name of the church), introduce in the early pages of the novel the theme of faith and doubt. They bring comfort to Christophe and nostalgia to his grandfather, Jean-Michel, a self-proclaimed "esprit fort." Christophe maintains an ambiguous attitude toward religion, nourished on the one hand by the indifference of his father and grandfather (and his own natural antipathy toward church ritual)

---

57. *Voyage intérieur*, p. 131.
58. Ibid., pp. 130–31.
59. Ibid., p. 187.

and on the other by his mother's unquestioning faith, his intuition of divinity in the world of nature, and the revelation of religious music which arouses him from his boredom, liberating his spirit from the prison of the church (p. 15). As long as he is a child, he manages to avoid any decisive resolution. Uncle Gottfried, his mother's brother, who later influences Christophe's attitude toward folk-music, helps at least to keep the question of faith alive in his mind by his equation of religion with the spirit of nature and music. He provides a correlation between the established church and Christophe's vague pantheism. In accordance with the pattern, the two religious crises of *Le Matin* affect Christophe's faith in contradictory ways. The death of his beloved grandfather, Jean-Michel, leaves the boy inconsolable despite the efforts of his uncle to reconcile him with his loss. Gottfried's passive faith is not adequate to the enormity of the occasion and acts as a trigger to Christophe's revolt against what seems to him God's injustice or caprice. In response to Gottfried's well-intentioned "Il faut se soumettre . . . . *Il* l'a voulu là-haut. Il faut aimer ce qu'*Il* veut," the boy cries out, "Je le déteste," although he takes fright and begins to pray with his uncle immediately afterward. The choice of words shows that this revolt is still an affirmation of belief, since it accepts the *reality* of God even if it does not acknowledge the implicit justice of his acts. Christophe's conception of the nature of God undergoes a complete change, however. From a neutral, passive presence which manages to infiltrate both the constriction of the church and the great expanse of nature, God becomes a malignant spirit ruling by fear and destruction, whose evil permeates the universe (p. 130). But this step backward in the development of the hero's faith has the effect of an almost immediate recoil in the direction of his Becoming. It affirms Christophe's will to struggle against the forces of destruction which threaten to engulf him, and it is a source of moral energy.

The death of Melchior, his father, accomplishes a further transformation of Christophe's attitude toward God, which the passage of time cannot sufficiently explain. Christophe cannot escape a feeling of complicity with the forces which led to the grotesque tragedy of his father's death by drowning while drunk. From his conviction of external evil lying in wait for men, he turns to a puritanical sense of his own potential evil, of internal forces which are even more dangerous, because of their subtlety and familiarity, than "la Bête aveugle." God is reinstated; the dialogue is reopened since He is no longer devoid of sense and responsibility. Christophe hears the voice of God encouraging him, answering his doubts about the sense of continuing to struggle when the final outcome must be death: "Allez mourir, vous qui devez mourir! Allez souffrir, vous qui devez souffrir! On ne vit pas pour être heureux. On vit pour accomplir ma Loi. Souffre. Meurs. Mais sois ce que tu dois être: —un Homme" (p. 221). This affirmation, which closes the book of Christophe's childhood before the tumult of adolescence, fore-shadows his succeeding evolution and announces the grandeur of the state of manhood. It presents God as a sympathetic but im-passive witness to the struggles of men in their Becoming. The goal which He acknowledges is not an ascension to the divine, but a secular fulfillment of the creative potential of man. There still re-mains, however, a link between the Creator and his creation, since the law of Becoming is His Law, imposed on men from without and enforced by the prestige of its source.

This thread is broken, however, by the ineluctable pattern of Christophe's law. The chapter which relates the young musician's first genuine religious experience is one of the most remarkable in the entire novel (pp. 241–50). It is entirely constructed of the con-flicting elements which mark Rolland's musical style. The first pages present in straightforward narrative the *status quo ante* of Christophe's faith, the ambiguity of his belief in the existence of God. He has put off taking account of his most intimate convictions. The violence of their fluctuations has not troubled him because of the preoccupations imposed on him by his family's situation and his role in it. In Rolland's words, "Au fond, il était trop religieux pour penser beaucoup à Dieu. Il vivait en Dieu, il n'avait pas besoin d'y croire" (p. 242). If he has a religious feeling when playing the church organ, he is not sure whether it is the music itself or its evo-cation of the Spirit: "Il était plus occupé de son orgue que de la messe, et plus religieux, les jours où la chapelle jouait du Bach que les jours où elle jouait du Mendelssohn" (p. 243). His need for sincerity with himself prevents him from accepting this unresolved question with cheerful equanimity, but his lack of education precludes answering it himself, and the people around him, laity and priest, have failed to give him any satisfactory response. Yet Christophe is unwilling to place himself under the spiritual authority of the Church fathers, just for the sake of avoiding the pangs of doubt.

Like Rolland's, Christophe's doubt reaches the critical state in early adolescence, under the catalytic effect of a change in environment and associations. Following the death of Melchior, Christophe and his mother move to an apartment more centrally located in town. There they come into contact with people whose personification of the traditional relationship between men and God is the focus of the crystallization of Christophe's personal beliefs. The Euler family, taken as a group, represents the Christianity of the German bourgeoisie: regularity in church attendance, strict observance of morality (and attention to that of neighbors), the necessary minimum of charity, and reverence for the formulas of devotion.

Christophe's crisis of conscience, however, is not precipitated just by these ambient circumstances. He has lived his life in them without having to confront the question of his faith decisively, and the change in his life is not in itself sufficient to produce that complete alteration of direction which characterizes the pattern of his progressive development. What is needed is the shock of a peculiar concatenation of environmental circumstance, physical atmosphere, psychological mood, and, in this case, the presence of one person to act as a trampoline against which he can take his rebounding motion. This role is taken by Leonhard Euler, a young man preparing for the clergy, to whom Christophe has turned for an explanation of his religious feelings.

The scene takes the form of a three-way dialogue between Leonhard, Christophe, and the setting; it is a counterpoint of rationalistic faith, searching man, and nature. Christophe finds himself existing alternately in two worlds, his consciousness being drawn inexorably toward the one which he feels to be more real. Leonhard's argument is composed of familiar elements: the ugliness of the world; the

comfort of renunciation; the beauty of eternal life; the evidence of
the Scriptures and tradition; the charitable power of prayer; the
satisfaction of believing for one who wants to believe and for whom
the fact of believing is evidence of Grace. Leonhard finally resorts
to the "Pari," which Christophe is not *honnête homme* enough to
appreciate.

During this exposition, which takes the form of questions and
answers between Christophe and Leonhard, a parallel dialogue takes
place between the musician and the world around him. It grows
in insistence as the passage progresses, gradually absorbing his attention. The scene is a cloister at dusk in a quiet spot which over-
looks the town, the misty countryside, and the Rhine flowing at the
base of the hill. Darkness gradually envelops them, hiding from
view the distant landscape, the Rhine, the town, the abandoned
graveyard nearby, and finally the two men. Simultaneously, Christophe experiences a heightened awareness of the sounds of nature
and of the life around him, obliterating the monologue which Leonhard, encouraged by Christophe's taciturnity, has not interrupted.

> Les grillons bruissaient sous les arbres du cimetière. Les cloches
> se mirent à sonner: la plus aiguë d'abord, toute seule, comme
> un oiseau plaintif, interrogea le ciel; puis la seconde, une tierce
> au-dessous, se mêla à sa plainte; enfin vint la plus grave à la
> quinte, qui semblait leur donner la réponse. Les trois voix se
> fondirent. C'était, au pied des tours, le bourdonnement d'une
> ruche grandiose. L'air et le coeur tremblaient. Christophe,
> retenant son souffle, pensait combien la musique des musiciens
> est pauvre auprès de cet océan de musique, où grondent des
> milliers d'êtres: c'est le faune sauvage, le libre monde des
> sons, auprès du monde domestique, catalogué, froidement
> étiqueté par l'intelligence humaine. Il se perdait dans cette
> immensité sonore, sans rivages et sans bornes. (pp. 248–49)

This musical emanation from the heart of living matter has no
difficulty in imposing itself on Christophe, sweeping away the
alternative which Leonhard represents. Yet Leonhard's exposition
of belief is essential to the movement of the scene. Without it Chris-

tophe would not have an idea to react against; the experience of nature would be passive and undefined. His resistance to the mediocre and shallow comfort which the future cleric propounds pushes him irrevocably into the stream of his mystical experience. His eventual reemergence into consciousness of time and place is only partial; he has left a vital part of himself in the ocean which he has glimpsed. As a result, it seems to him that he has reawakened in a world different from the one he left. The difference is his loss of faith; the world is the same, but God has disappeared from it. Rolland describes this not as a retrogressive movement, but as a "coup de la grâce." The inadequate conception of divinity is erased, and in its place Christophe feels an emotion which might be either anguish or rapture: "Il avait la sensation soudaine du vaste monde, brûlant, sauvage, incommensurable . . . le monde qui déborde Dieu!" (p. 250). This provisional rejection of God in the frame of reference of Christophe's Becoming is a necessary enlargement and validation of the creative experience toward which he is moving through the entire novel. It turns away from accepted forms and toward the life-force itself.

One of the frequent *intermezzi* in the stream of the novel's development completes the parallel between Christophe's adolescent religious experience and Rolland's in this angular progression. Here the young hero has an "éclair" which corresponds with Rolland's revelation of Spinoza. Christophe is sitting in his room, trying desperately to arrive at some answer to the questions into which the loss of his faith has plunged him, reading theological, scientific, and philosophical texts, penetrated by anguish at the thought of the abyss into which he is falling. The revelation does not come from a book in this case, but the experience is the same—that of a God present in all substance, in Christophe himself, who overflows the limitations placed on him by Christianity and enlarges the definition of man at the same time. Christophe is filled with the idea that God is in him, as he is in God; that he *is* God, thanks to his immersion in the force of life. The language of this mystical crisis is evocative of the rising and falling pattern which characterizes Christophe's spiritual life: his movement is downward, breathtaking, dizzying, into the watery flow which is the image of the all-penetrating life-force. Here it combines with Renan's "route en lacets" to produce a cataract and an eddy.

> Le monde se ruait en Lui, comme une cataracte. Dans l'horreur et l'extase de cet effondrement, Christophe tombait aussi, emporté par le tourbillon qui broyait comme des pailles les lois de la nature. Il avait perdu le souffle, il était ivre de cette chute en Dieu . . . Dieu-abîme! Dieu-gouffre, Brasier de l'Etre! Ouragan de la vie! (p. 264)

Even this phase of his progress, which represents an obvious rising trend both in the traditional context of man's spiritual ascension toward God and in that of Christophe's progression toward his apotheosis at the novel's end, is initiated by a rebounding movement. The new élan plunges Christophe into the flowing substance of the life-force. Paradoxically, this passage illustrates the jagged path of Christophe's development in another way: the *trop-plein* of this mystical experience of life stifles creativity and represents a negative step in his artistic progress which is reversed only by a succeeding experience of death. Although numerous other examples could be cited of this pattern at work in the narrative structure of the novel, it will suffice to note here two cases in which the mountain road takes on reality as image as well as geometric pattern. Typically, these passages occur at important articulations in the narrative and in the hero's spiritual and artistic development.

At the end of *Dans la Maison* (pp. 1084–86), which is devoted to Christophe's discovery of the "house" of France and his efforts to renew, through the spirit of his music, the cultural bonds which link its separate chambers, the hero receives news of his mother's illness and returns to Germany in time to see her die. A fugitive from justice because of events which led him to leave Germany earlier, Christophe rejoins his friend Olivier at the Franco-German border, and once in French territory, they set out to return to Paris. As in several other similar points of the narrative, Christophe chooses to make part of the journey on foot (Cf. pp. 314, 582): Rolland uses this device to make the reader more aware of the symbolic function of the ground covered, its association of space, time, and life-flow.

In this case, the road leads to a clearing at the summit of a hill, which looks out over a valley on the German side of the border. Here, looking back at the land from which he has come, with its memories of dead friends and relations, Christophe arrives at a new vision. It goes beyond the national and "racial" concerns of the preceding volumes and redefines the function of the composer's art in terms of a broader common denominator: the unenfranchised "little" people of the earth. In one sense, this is a return to a creative phase through which Christophe passed much earlier in *L'Aube*. But in the transcendent dialectic of his Becoming, the base on which this new popular aesthetic rests is both wider and deeper, thanks to Christophe's emotional and artistic experiences during the interval. This change of direction is the sum of all the reversals which have preceded it.

Like all reversals, this one implies a negation: Christophe rises above the struggle for success and recognition in the "feverish and sterile world" of Parisian culture, as well as the search for a national artistic identity for his country of adoption. But the positive aspect of the turn is the one which Rolland emphasizes. Christophe returns to things and people with whom he has momentarily lost contact. It is significant, as we shall see in the next chapter, that this past is represented here solely by the dead: his mother, Gottfried, Schulz, Sabine, and Antoinette. An important part of the impulsion toward new things which moves Christophe is given by the departed spirits he carries with him. To underline this connection, Rolland cites a tercet from Dante's *Inferno* (XXIII, 1–3) as epigraph at the end of the volume.

A similar passage at the end of *Le Buisson ardent* (pp. 1415–26) takes Rolland's hero to Alpine heights after the death of Olivier and the end of an adulterous love affair which almost brings Christophe and his mistress to suicide. Distraught and drained of will by his experience, he waits in a mountain retreat for death to come. Then, one day, he takes a walk, whose many changes of direction and setting symbolize at the same time his moral confusion and the various temptations to which he is open in his current state of emptiness. In the valley, he finds villages suggestive of pastoral peace and bells ringing for Easter week. Turning away, he seeks the heights and finds a sanatorium in which a well-known author, now insane, tells him he is waiting for the Resurrection. In a hallucinatory daze, Christophe passes through a dead forest reminiscent of Flaubert's *Saint-Julien* or Dante's *selva oscura* in its mysterious density. Upon his emergence into the light, he feels the eerie stillness of the air broken by a wind which suddenly arises, the springtime wind of the Alps, the *foehn,* which penetrates and possesses him, restoring life and the power of creation.

This "resurrection" represents a new spiritual and artistic direction. Turning away from the comforts of peace and tranquillity and the temptation of Christian consolation, Christophe enters a phase in which his music is a direct, irrational transcription of the emotional storm awakened in him by the *foehn*. He becomes the will-less instrument of the restorative power of spring rebirth. Rolland cites Goethe's testimony to the "ineffable enigma of the world and life," the *demoniacal* force (p. 1425) which overcame him in moments of creative frenzy. Rolland underlines the significance of this symbolic image as change and reversal at the end of *Le Buisson ardent*. There the mountain path is transformed into the flight of a lark: "Et l'âme de Christophe était comme l'alouette. Elle savait qu'elle retomberait tout à l'heure, et bien des fois encore. Mais elle savait aussi qu'infatigablement elle remonterait dans le feu" (p. 1428).

The presence of the theme of death in these illustrations of Rolland's use of the mountain path pattern and image is obviously not coincidental. In Christophe's Becoming, symbolic and real death play an important role which reflects Rolland's long preoccupation with the idea and certain literary influences which contributed to the formulation of his novel's structure.

The Death Urge and Creation: Goethe's "Stirb und werde"

The theme of death plays a remarkable role in the pattern of Jean-Christophe's artistic and spiritual development. This is evident in Christophe's earliest experiences as a child. Examination of Rolland's personal writings reveals the intimate source of this influence on the life of his fictional character. The author was haunted by the idea of death in his earliest memories. He lived under its shadow from infancy, when a negligent servant-girl left him uncovered in the open air one day in winter. He was fortunate to survive, but his lungs were weakened for life, and he had to be on guard constantly against the threat of tuberculosis. The impression of death's imminence which hangs over Rolland's diary of the Ecole Normale persists through the letters and diary of the succeeding two decades: Rolland would not then have believed that he would only be overtaken by his enemy and companion at the age of seventy-eight.

Rolland's experience with death in its action upon the circle of his family and friends may not have been greater than the norm imposed on the general run of men by the human condition, but there can be no doubt of the deep effect this experience had on his thinking. His encounters with death came at crucial moments. His sister Madeleine, the namesake of a surviving younger sister, died when he was five years old, and her image of otherworldly tenderness and prophetic distance haunted his later life. Georges Mille's death in September 1888 came when Rolland had arrived at a deep sense of communion with his fellow student in the "Cloître de la rue d'Ulm"—a communion equaled only by the long standing one with André Suarès—and when he was under the premonition of his own imminent passing: Rolland's reaction to the news, received during a vacation in the Alps, is suggestive of several scenes in the novel.[60] Malwida von Meysenbug died in 1903, culminating the touching friendship of a very young man and a very old woman, during which the specter had made its presence felt on both sides because of ill health. Her death came at a moment in the emotional life of the author when, as a result of the failure of his marriage to Clotilde Bréal, his courage was threatened. More remote, but adding weight to his experience, were the death of Victor Hugo, in whose massive funeral rites Rolland participated as an adolescent; that of Leo Tolstoy, the guiding figure of his early manhood, which

60. *Cloître*, pp. 252–57.

coincided with a serious automobile accident that brought Rolland forcibly into immediate contact with his personal demon; and that of Charles Péguy, his editor and comrade-in-arms at the turn of the century, from whom his path had since diverged. His passing was certainly submerged by the immense slaughter which had already begun in Europe, but Rolland still paid eloquent and heartfelt tribute to Péguy in an article sent to the *Journal de Genève*. Perhaps it took the unbridled massacre of the First World War to exorcize the demon of death, but certainly, up to that point, Rolland's work is haunted by it, and that "hantise" is an integral element of his moral and aesthetic philosophy.

A parallel can be drawn between the development of death as a literary theme in Rolland's conception of the creative artist's Becoming and the evolution of his opinion concerning the works and, more importantly, the personality of Goethe. It is difficult to say if Goethe's writings exerted an influence on Rolland's thinking, but it may be useful to show how the German author's rising attraction for Rolland was symptomatic of an important development in his thought. The turning point in this progression came about at a critical juncture in Rolland's life, following the death of Malwida von Meysenbug and the end of his marriage, just as *Jean-Christophe* was beginning to take concrete shape. In addition, Goethe provided the author with the kind of metaphoric expression around which Rolland's thinking tended to formulate itself in architectural lines: the "Stirb und werde" which Rolland took as the title of his later tribute to the German poet.

In later years, Rolland attempted to define Goethe's influence on himself: in an article on the German poet,[61] he pays tribute to the universality and indefinability of Goethe's genius, his dedication to truth, and his intuitional penetration of life and nature, which coincided with Rolland's own view of the artistic process:

> Ses passions, ses créations, son activité sociale et scientifique, toute cette gerbe d'être dont l'oeuvre poétique forme le coeur, tout est lié, rien ne s'écarte des directions que l'architecte de la vie a dessinées. Qui, l'architecte? La volonté arbitraire de l'âme

61. First published in *Europe* (Apr. 15, 1932), and later in *Compagnons de route*.

isolée? Non, la Nature . . . dont cet homme est un fragment, de même substance, soumis aux lois qui la commandent, mais conscient.[62]

This endorsement of Goethe, however, represents his admission into the circle of Rolland's idols after its original definition. To judge by the opinions on Goethe found in Rolland's diary and correspondence prior to *Jean-Christophe* Goethe was a latecomer, whose acceptance was based on Rolland's reinterpretation of his works and biography. Although his name figures frequently in *Le Cloître de la rue d'Ulm,* especially in the *Credo quia verum,* where it is associated with Renan's among the models for ironic detachment, Goethe's presence seems to have resulted from Suarès' estimation, which Rolland tacitly accepted, rather than from his personal conviction. Since the *Credo* was addressed to Suarès, Rolland wished to express himself in his friend's philosophical vocabulary. There is little evidence of Rolland's penetration of, or by, the works of Goethe at this point.

This impression is substantiated by the correspondence between Rolland and Malwida von Meysenbug. Scattered through it is a running dialogue between the "Idealistin" and her young friend on the subject of Goethe, whom Malwida idolized. The first object that had struck Rolland's attention upon entering her apartment in Rome was an imposing bust of Goethe. Practically from that moment on, there arose between them one of the few basic controversies in their relationship. Malwida tried incessantly to convert the young man to her opinion, and Rolland, with a great show of goodwill, resisted stubbornly. His attitude toward Goethe then, expressed in letters to his mother, certainly does not accord with the picture he gives of him in 1932.

Ce sensualisme froid, cet égoïsme artistique, cette nature pondérée, machine à écrire esthétiquement ses sentiments et ses sensations, ne sont pas de mon goût. Une seule chose m'a toujours fasciné en lui, la puissance de volonté sur lui-même; mais à la condition de ne pas étouffer la spontanéité de l'âme et l'éclat des passions.[63]

62. *Compagnons de route,* pp. 103–04.
63. *Retour au Palais Farnèse,* p. 65 (Nov. 1890).

This initial view persists until the belated reevaluation reflected in Rolland's writings from 1901 on. Oddly, it is not the long argument with his esteemed friend Malwida which changed his mind. After a series of references to their difference of opinion the subject gradually disappeared from their correspondence by mutual consent (as did the subject of another disagreement, the Dreyfus affair). Rather, the turning point in his attitude is associated with the period of emotional instability which followed his divorce from Clotilde Bréal and which saw Rolland, in his search for spiritual calm, turning toward the friendship of his adolescent love, Sofia Bertolini. Rather than Goethe's works, it is Eckermann's *Conversations with Goethe* which accomplished the change. A letter to Sofia acknowledges the parallelism of the two new influences in his life:

> Au bienfait apaisant de votre influence sur mon coeur s'est ajoutée celle de Goethe sur mon esprit. J'en ai beaucoup lu depuis un mois, surtout les conversations avec Eckermann, que vous devez connaître et qui sont un de mes livres de prédilection. Je puis dire que j'ai vécu intimement avec lui, et qu'il a grandement affermi mon calme et éclairé ma volonté.[64]

These readings gave him, for the first time, the insight into Goethe which characterizes his appraisal of him from that time and which enters into the description of Christophe's final creative stage. Goethe ceased to be "an Olympian idol." Certain passages of Eckermann's conversations revealed to Rolland Goethe's consciousness of the frightening abysses of the irrational and his fascination with Oriental philosophy, which he resisted because of his fear of it.[65] The discovery, through the *Conversations,* of Goethe's admiration for Spinoza and of the latter's influence on the scene of the "Mothers" in the second *Faust* no doubt contributed to this new kinship of minds, which may be seen in a letter of September 1904 (*Jean-Christophe*

64. *Chère Sofia,* I, 19 (Sept. 1901).
65. Rolland later drew a parallel between this resistance and that which Goethe practiced toward Beethoven's music, for fear of succumbing to its destructive influence over his will—a reaction shared by Tolstoy in his latter years, at the time of *What Is Art?* See Romain Rolland, *Goethe et Beethoven* (Paris, Editions du Sablier, 1930), pp. 118–19.

was well under way: Rolland was completing *L'Adolescent*): "La grandeur de Goethe fut justement qu'il réussit à faire régner la paix et la lumière dans une âme, qui, jusqu'à sa vieillesse, fut pleine d'étranges replis, et d'ombres inquiètes." [66]

The trait of Goethe's artistic personality which struck Rolland most powerfully in the *Conversations* was the theme of death in the creative process. Rolland's article on Goethe is dominated by the idea of the writer's indefinability, the transient stage of his artistic personality which each of his works represents. Goethe constantly progressed in his creation by destroying in himself, by "discharging" electrically, the present ideal for the sake of the succeeding one:

> C'est que presque chaque oeuvre—à part l'oeuvre de toute la vie: *Faust*—est de passage, comme on dit en musique. Et le créateur, qui s'y décharge de ses électricités contraires, passe et s'élève, de l'une à l'autre dissonance, vers la plus haute et plus pleine harmonie, qui toujours le fuit, mais, le fuyant, l'attire en haut, toujours plus haut.[67]

The source for this appraisal of Goethe's artistic progress can be found in numerous passages of the *Conversations*. One may be taken as typical: after an evening of music, during which the wife of Goethe's composer-friend Eberwein sang some musical settings of the *West-östlicher Divan,* Goethe confided to Eckermann his sense of divorce from these works of his not-too-distant past:

> Nachdem die Gesellschaft gegangen, blieb ich noch einige Augenblicke mit Goethe allein. "Ich habe," sagte er, "diesen Abend die Bemerkung gemacht, dass diese Lieder des 'Divan' gar kein Verhältnis mehr zu mir haben. Sowohl was darin orientalisch als was darin leidenschaftlich ist, hat aufgehört in mir fortzuleben; es ist wie eine abgestreifte Schlangenhaut am Wege liegen geblieben.[68]

Ironically Rolland selected a motto from one of the poems in this "outworn" collection, *Selige Sehnsucht,* as the motif for this element

66. *Chère Sofia, 1,* 195.
67. *Compagnons de route,* pp. 105–06.
68. *Gespräche mit Goethe, 1,* 202–03 (1827).

of Goethe's personality, which had the strongest influence on his personal appraisal of the writer:

> J'ai dit, en commençant ces pages, que chacun prend dans l'immense champ de la pensée, que représente l'oeuvre et la vie de Goethe, ce qui s'apparente à son essence personnelle. J'ai pris ce mot:
> —"*Meurs et deviens!*"
> Il est central dans l'âme de Goethe—s'il n'est pas l'unique foyer.[69]

The poem, which symbolizes the aspirations of the truly living— that is to say, the creative—person by the fatal attraction of the flame for the moth, takes the image of the "resurrection of the flesh" which irresistibly draws the lover back to his beloved following his "death." It ends in a strophe which insists on the necessity of this desire for death in creation and beauty if one is to avoid mediocrity and unproductiveness on earth:

> Und so lang du das nicht hast,
> Dieses: Stirb und werde!
> Bist du nur ein trüber Gast
> Auf der dunklen Erde.

There can be no doubt about the psychological relevance of this poem to the era in Rolland's life when he underwent Goethe's influence: his rebirth to a new life following the death of his marriage and his rededication to literature under the aegis of the "heroic lives," *Beethoven* and *Jean-Christophe.* This date also coincides with Rolland's turning away from the theater. His most concentrated period of creation in the medium of historical drama, *Les Tragédies de la Foi* and *Le Théâtre de la Révolution,* now lay behind him. Although no equivalent example of artistic "Death and Becoming" is to be found in his life and work previous to this era, from this time on Rolland underwent similar periodic renewals of his art implying the negation of what had gone before. The transition from the heroic idealism of *Jean-Christophe* to the *gauloiserie* of *Colas Breugnon* saw such a spiritual death and rebirth:

---

69. *Compagnons de route,* p. 107.

> Comme tout artiste vraiment vivant, je suis en incessante évolution. On peut même dire que chaque fois que j'ai exprimé une passion, un état d'âme, j'en suis délivré, et que des passions différentes veulent à leur tour surgir. C'est une loi.[70]

This is reflected in a profound sense of spiritual anxiety in the journal of the previous year, during an interregnum between negation of the past and the foundation of a new phase:

> Je suis las de moi, de ma misérable enveloppe. J'ai usé mon instrument. Mon corps chétif est brisé. Mon âme même ne me suffit plus. . . . Mon Dieu, tu me détruis. Pourquoi me plaindre? Tu t'es servi de moi. Je t'ai servi. Brise-moi, et prends un autre instrument, plus fort et meilleur. J'ai hâte moi-même de n'être plus, afin de revenir à toi.[71]

If the tendencies which produced this peculiar aspect of the creative life were latent in Rolland before this emergence, it seems nevertheless undeniable that Goethe's life and the motto from his work which Rolland incorporated into his vocabulary of motives were instrumental in the conscious realization of their function as law in his life and that of his musician-hero. He accorded these words an exalted place when, speaking of them as "l'unique foyer" of Goethe's thought, he added: "Puisque ma vie y a, cent fois, ranimé sa propre flamme, qu'on me permette de l'attiser! Je veux montrer le Goethe de ce brasier . . . celui-ci est le mien. Il m'a nourri." [72]

The fact that Goethe was a greater artist than Renan must have counted in the development of the novel. While their influences on the creative personality of Jean-Christophe are often parallel, the areas of his personality in which each has the most relevancy may be fairly clearly distinguished. Goethe's influence seems most active in the movement of Christophe through the various stages of his artistic, rather than emotional or moral, development. Each of these stages is characterized by a denial, a renunciation, of those preceding it. It is not simply a case of linear development or elaboration

---

70. *Correspondance entre Louis Gillet et Romain Rolland,* p. 284.
71. *De Jean-Christophe à Colas Breugnon,* p. 142.
72. *Compagnons de route,* p. 107.

of a simple material into a more complex or more valid one. Every
new period of his artistic Becoming is accompanied by the death,
the deliberate sacrifice, of what has gone before. Christophe does
not simply abandon the outmoded style or point of view—it must
be excised, frequently at great emotional cost. As he casts off these
successive cloaks of his creative personality, he experiences shame,
scorn, or hatred for what he has been. A sense of detachment from
what he has created makes his past works seem the product of
someone entirely foreign. His experience of this for the first time,
under the influence of his uncle Gottfried, is a renunciation of artistic
pride for a popularly inspired music. The succeeding evolution,
described in *Sables mouvants,* is in the direction of sincerity in
passion as the only proper source of valid inspiration:

> Le dégoût que lui inspirèrent ses compositions anciennes, pro-
> duites sans passion, fit qu'avec son exagération coutumière, il
> décida de ne plus rien écrire qu'il ne fût contraint d'écrire par
> une nécessité passionnée; et, laissant là sa poursuite aux idées,
> il jura de renoncer pour toujours à la musique, si la création ne
> s'imposait, à coups de tonnerre. (p. 381)

Later, as his success becomes established by past works (even of
the immediate past), Christophe is annoyed rather than pleased by
this tribute, which no longer seems relevant to himself, to his present
artistic personality. When he learns of the applause which greeted
the performance of a work already a year old, he is surprised and
disgusted:

> Il haussait les épaules, et disait qu'on le laissât tranquille. Il
> eût compris qu'on applaudît le *David,* l'année précédente, quand
> il l'avait écrit; mais maintenant il en était loin, il avait gravi
> quelques échelons de plus. Volontiers, il eût dit aux gens qui
> lui parlaient de son ancienne oeuvre:
> —Laissez-moi tranquille avec cette ordure! Elle me dégoûte.
> (p. 1074)

Subsequent development brings a denial of the above-mentioned
sincerity in passion. Under the influence of his love for the actress

Françoise Oudon, who impresses on him the need for communication between the creator and his audience, Christophe evolves a new conception of the artist's role:

> Son idéal était le vivant objectivisme de l'aède, qui se dépouille de soi, pour vêtir les passions collectives qui soufflent sur le monde . . . . La musique moderne qui parle tant de soi et fait à tout venant ses confidences indiscrètes est un manque de pudeur et un manque de goût. (p. 1175)

This view even contradicts, momentarily, the basis of his previous scorn for his past works. It demands immediate communication between creator and public, a communication he had turned his back on because of the public's inability to comprehend him. Rejecting the subjectivism of nineteenth-century *lieder,* whose tradition he had been following, he attempts to rejoin the objective current of the eighteenth century. It is curious that this new attitude reveals itself in a rehabilitation of the musical tastes proposed by Goethe for the settings of his lyric poems by his friend Zelter—although Zelter and Goethe's collaboration represented to Rolland, at the time of *Beethoven,* the antithesis of all that his hero stood for. Thus this phase of Christophe's art repudiates a direction in music initiated by Beethoven, his supposed model. This repudiation is equivalent to total condemnation of his work up to that moment. Each successive stage of Christophe's development, by this violent reversal of values, is a symbolic killing of the man he has been.

The recurrence of the death theme in *Jean-Christophe* is too insistent to be regarded as less than a vital element of development. The superabundance of life which swells in the hero's body and spirit translates itself at moments of crisis into a powerful death urge: e.g. young Christophe's attempt to commit suicide by strangling himself, out of sheer indignation at the injustice of his schoolmaster's treatment of him (p. 47). For a period of two or three years in his youth, Christophe is haunted by terrors associated with falling, night, obscure corners, closed rooms, and turns in the road. To supplement this baggage of childhood fears, the unexpected death of a playmate, Fritz, destroys his reassuring association of death with old age, as does his discovery that, somewhat like the author, he has lost a brother, a namesake who died in infancy. Paradoxically, yet in accordance with this scheme of movement, out of this intimate contact with death is evolved Christophe's intense desire to create, to express in some way the irresistible force within and around him before his annihilation. Reflecting Rolland's diary, he cries out when he is in terror of death's imminence, "Oh! que je vive seulement . . . jusqu'à dix-huit ans!" (p. 57).[73] His dread of death is transformed into an antidote against its fascination. His rage and fear at the thought of dying before realizing the latent power within him balance his disgust with life, which is strong enough to bring him to the brink of suicide. These two facets of the theme are brought into focus in a scene of *L'Adolescent* where Christophe almost commits suicide by drowning himself in the river, whose symbolism of the life-force acts obscurely to save him.

This scheme of action and reaction through the intervention of death informs the entire novel. Christophe's "compagnons de route" tend to influence him and his art as profoundly by their deaths as by their contacts in life. His grandfather's violent seizure by apoplexy not only stirs in him feelings of revolt but reveals to him the pain and suffering inherent in the life of man:

> On croyait vivre, on croyait avoir quelque expérience de la vie: on voit qu'on ne savait rien . . . . Tout le langage humain, toute la sagesse humaine, n'est qu'un guignol de raides automates, auprès de l'éblouissement funèbre de la réalité,—ces misérables êtres de boue et de sang, dont tout le vain effort est de fixer une vie, qui pourrit d'heure en heure. (p. 130)

Christophe does not turn away from the stream of reality whose horror is proved by this absurdity, the death of a man who was an embodiment of physical joy. His experience immerses him more fully in it and makes him embrace bodily the opponent with whom he must struggle in his efforts to create. The touch of death, so

73. Cf. *Cloître*, pp. 175, 180, 188.

near to his person and his heart, reinforces his commitment to life through the intuitive faculties which partake substantively in its flow and form the link between artist and nature. Jean-Michel's death also consecrates his grandson's inheritance of the obligations of musical talent: it sends him out to provide for his family and marks a real beginning of the young musician's struggle to make his way in the world of men.

Similarly, the death of his father Melchior marks a turning point in Christophe's moral progress, reestablishing a balance in his relationship with his family, which the friction between father and son had upset and which his first experience of love almost destroyed. The family tie, the "bloodstream," takes on the symbolism of participation in the stream of existence. Melchior's death reaffirms Christophe's sense of involvement in the life-stream, strengthening his determination to be the instrument of its further evolution, fulfilling more positively the gifts which his father squandered. The latter's death inaugurates a period of feverish creative labor and of increased bitterness in Christophe's contacts with the world around him, rather than of withdrawal into himself. When this impulsion is again lost after a sequence of emotional crises brought on by love affairs, the restoration is accomplished by a series of contacts with death: a hallucination in which Christophe sees Melchior's spirit; a haunting scene in which his uncle Gottfried, finding him drunk, persists in addressing him by his father's name; and a visit to his father's grave at the end of *L'Adolescent* (pp. 369–71).

The pattern established by these first experiences with death is followed throughout the life of the musician. After a period of emotional torpor, Christophe receives from these losses an impulsion toward life, a new vigor and desire to create, to negate death. The example of Sabine's death is typical: overwhelmed at first by its injustice, Christophe finds himself gradually seized by the life-force welling up inside him, the powerful rhythm of nature which drowns out the voice of his mourning. Even when he visits the country cemetery where she is buried, his sense of communion is dispelled by the evidences of life around him, the scenes of nature which irresistibly draw his attention:

> En dépit de son deuil, son coeur battait des rythmes allègres
> et violents; des chants emportés bondissaient sur des mètres
> ivres; tout célébrait la vie; la tristesse même prenait un caractère
> de fête. . . . Et triste, l'âme pleine de mort et le corps plein de
> vie, il s'abandonna à sa force renaissante, à la joie délirante et
> absurde de vivre. (p. 317)

The experience at close hand of death's pain and injustice, its
contradiction of the aspirations of life, is necessary to the hero's
movement, providing momentum at times when he is becoming
stagnant. The absurdity of life, which death seems to prove, is not a
valid argument against participation in it; the grip of life on man is
irrational, Dionysian, "delirious," irresistible, invulnerable to the
assaults of reason. One is reminded here of Renan's description, in
the preface to *L'Abbesse de Jouarre,* of the early Christians' emotional excesses on the eve of their martyrdom and of the Abbess'
surrender to sensuality just prior to her execution during the Terror.
Christophe's reaction is an example of the increased awareness of the
life-force given by death's imminence or its presence in the surrounding world.

Rolland, until the end of the novel, uses the death of Jean-
Christophe's family and friends as his chief transitional device or
modulation, just as he utilizes his hero's death as the final transition
or cadence. Each of these experiences inaugurates a new movement
in the novel, if one takes that musical term to mean mood or dominant sentiment—and, by extension, definition of the composer's art—
rather than tempo or rhythm. As we have seen, death is symbolic
of some aspect of the hero's creative personality which is being displaced or surpassed. It provides a new vision and therefore creates
or inspires a new pattern of life and art. Consistent with this function is the fact that, in the general dialectic pattern of Christophe's
development, each successive experience with death tends to negate
the one immediately preceding it.

Uncle Gottfried's death, for example, produces a less violent reaction in Christophe than Sabine's, which precedes it (*La Révolte,* pp.
582 ff.). This is not merely an accident but a manifestation of the

pattern of alternation. The entire episode is presented in a way which involves the hero less directly: Christophe, in one of his symbolic walks, discovers the house in which his uncle, an itinerant merchant, has died recently. He finds a blind girl living there, in whom Gottfried had restored hope by teaching her to concentrate on the beautiful sounds of life. The hero has a revelation of the illusions of German optimism, symbolized by the blind girl. His artistic reaction is toward a new realism based on a passionate acceptance of truth and refusal of illusory consolations. Although Rolland does not make the application of this "realism" to music entirely clear, he does at least use it as an impulsion of his hero away from German culture and toward France and its rational, analytic spirit in art and music.

If Christophe's intellectual movement toward France is initiated by Gottfried's death, his violent flight from Germany results from an incident in that series of blood-rages, starting with his near-suicide in *L'Aube,* which leads ultimately to his killing of a soldier in the political riots of *Le Buisson ardent* (p. 1325). Christophe's defense of some peasants from the bullying of a squadron of soldiers leads to a brawl in which one of the soldiers is badly wounded, and sends the hero into exile in France (*La Révolte,* pp. 612 ff.). In this passage, the brutal violence which comes close to murder is coupled thematically, as in several other passages of the novel, with amorous passion, the hero's life-force, and its expression in musical creation (Cf. *L'Adolescent,* pp. 268–69).

The remaining instances in *Jean-Christophe* where death serves as a turning point in the hero's development have similar effects: the resilience of a soul which has lost its mobility, a renewal of its artistic progress after some detour, or a slight alteration in its apparent direction while still maintaining the upward movement. Christophe's brush with death during a serious illness in volume two of *La Foire sur la Place* reveals to him his solitude in Paris and initiates his artistic and social involvement in the life of its simple people—one of whom has saved his life by her attentions. These events are critical in the establishment of one of Christophe's major artistic periods, during which, under the influence of Tolstoy and the popular-theater movement, he searches for the wellsprings of French music in the people. We have already seen the effect on Christophe's life and art of the deaths of his mother and Olivier.

In contrast with this entire series, however, stands the death of Grazia in *La Nouvelle Journée*. Whereas the earlier experiences with death have all acted as impulsions to movement, points of rebound, this death alone, before Christophe's own, is characterized by a leveling off. This transformation is not so much a reaction to previous direction as a diffusion of the movement of the hero's life, prefiguring his arrival at union with the eternal. This change is prepared for in the novel by the effect of the musician's love for Grazia. Christophe "becomes classic," arriving at a point where his music, in its communion with the stream of being, can express not only its durational movement but its motionless totality. His music, although representing a mere point in the stream of musical history, is nonetheless an emanation of the composer's timeless intuition. It is characterized by an atmosphere of light and peace, taking its inspiration from that peculiar quality which Rolland found in Italian art. In an ironic transposition of Rolland's primal vision of the novel, Christophe achieves this intuition on the Janicular Hill in the final period of his life (p. 1561). The composer-hero turns to a time-defying eclecticism which nourishes its creative instinct on the "classical" creations of all civilizations, nationalities, and eras.

Grazia's death does not alter this pattern but consecrates it by acting as a crystallizing agent, fixing Christophe's development on a plateau of peace. There is no revolt in Christophe's reception of the news of his friend's death: the scene in which he reads the letter informing him of the event illustrates the new stage which he has reached. He remains calm and continues a discussion with friends without relating the news to them. Only his leaving the room without explanation for a few minutes reveals to the reader the emotion which he undergoes. Rolland indicates in *Le Voyage intérieur* a source of this scene and of Christophe's personality at this stage: the moments when Malwida von Meysenbug, in her later illness, unobtrusively left Rolland's company for fear of inflicting the sight of her suffering on him. That chapter, "Amore, Pace," provides further proof of the influence of the image of Italy on the final stages in the hero's accession toward union with eternity.

Rolland's manner of shaping the life of his hero is not entirely changed at this point. His tendency to manipulate his character in terms of movement and Becoming is too basic to be denied even here. The pattern of transcendence through resilience is attenuated by this near-accession to immortality, but as long as there is life in the hero, he must continue to reflect change and mobility in his progression toward death. The influence of the "plateau" persists for a few months but naturally loses its strength through absence of movement. Therefore Christophe undergoes a last change before the final impetus which raises him to eternity. More than movement, this change is an attenuation of the mood which Grazia's death has evoked—a loss of concentration after its artistic realization in a series of eclectic works reflecting stoical inspiration: a musical setting of the scene between Mary Magdalene and the gardener in the Gospels, a group of songs based on popular Spanish *cantares,* and two symphonies entitled *L'Ile des Calmes* and *Le Songe de Scipion:*

> Cet *"enthousiasme que produit le désespoir, au moment d'une grande perte,"* dura un ou deux mois. Après quoi Christophe reprit son rang dans la vie, d'un coeur robuste et d'un pas assuré. Le vent de la mort avait soufflé les derniers brouillards du pessimisme, le gris de l'âme stoïcienne, et les fantasmagories du clair-obscur mystique. (p. 1558)

The course of his day-to-day life continues on a less exalted level, but Grazia's death has prepared his moral equilibrium for the final leap which, in accordance with the pattern of transcendence given by the series of deaths through which he has lived and to complete the cycle initiated with his birth, brings Christophe's apotheosis in death.

A letter of October 1912 bears witness both to the emotion aroused in Rolland's public by the death of his hero and to the author's conviction that his novel required it for a variety of reasons and on a number of levels. Answering J.-R. Bloch's letter of "condolence," Rolland wrote:

> Er starb, ein Mensch wie alle . . . J'ai connu votre douleur chaque fois que j'ai vu mourir un des grands que j'ai aimés: Tolstoy, Wagner, Beethoven . . . (car je les ai *vus* mourir). Je l'ai connue lorsque j'ai vu tomber Siegfried, à la fin de la quatrième journée du Ring, à Bayreuth . . . . Il le faut. *Es muss sein* . . . . Un Christophe ne peut pas tricher avec la mort. Et puis, c'est bien ainsi. Il faut que Christophe meure avec la génération qu'il incarne, pour que la vie nouvelle puisse librement fleurir.[74]

Christophe's "Kunsttod"

One may add to Christophe's musical attributes the fact that, like many operatic heroes, he spends an inordinate time dying. This reflects Rolland's fascination with the spiritual processes involved in the culminating moments of life.[75] The death agony provides an opportunity to recapitulate the movements of life in the hour when all is defined: Christophe's spiritual elevation permits him to gaze down the tortuous path he has followed "comme une succession d'étages" and to evaluate each crisis, each apparent regression, in his upward movement. This is also, however, the final realization of an attitude which permeates the entire book and its definition of the creative life. Death is the end of life in a double sense, and the artist seeking communion with life's essential stream must keep death present in his mind. Rolland pays homage in *Le Seuil* to the duality of corporeal and spiritual in the act of death, its summation of the duality in man's nature: "Ta puanteur est saine." [76] Death is a threshold, *the* threshold: it is not a "way out," but the entrance into a larger life, not a painless exit into bliss, but the mortally agonizing narrow gate into the unknown.

It is in accordance with this simultaneous idealization of the mys-

---

74. *Deux hommes se rencontrent*, p. 149.
75. Cf. for example the chapter intended for *Le Voyage intérieur* published in 1945 as *Le Seuil* and the final book of *L'Ame enchantée*.
76. *Le Seuil*, p. 74.

tical nature of death and concentration on its carnal pain and squalidness that Rolland describes the death of Jean-Christophe. The hero, who has lived with death and communed with it in his creation, experiences in constantly changing fashion the effects of its dichotomous properties. The hallucinated dialogue with Death and with the Spirit which has characterized Christophe's moments of communion in creation is here carried to its climax and fruition. The symbol of the river which opened the novel and carried the hero past the landmarks—castles, vineyards, and towns—which represented his passing contacts with external reality is here expressed in parallel with the image of the "route en lacets." As the latter brought Christophe, in his irregular ascension toward the Spirit, to a plateau with the death of Grazia, so in the moment of his death Christophe sees the river, near the terminal point which is its source, its "final cause," broadening out and losing its individual definition as it merges with the ocean, that sea of Being evoked by the "éclair de Spinoza":

> Christophe . . . vit, le fleuve débordé, couvrant les champs, roulant auguste, lent, presque immobile. Et, comme une lueur d'acier, au bord de l'horizon, semblait courir vers lui une ligne de flots d'argent, qui tremblaient au soleil. Le bruit de l'Océan. (pp. 1592–93)

Closer than ever before to the eternal witness of life and art, the composer continues his dialogue, alternately challenging, complaining, and submitting in the throes of this final resolution. Born out of this verbal dialogue is a parallel in music which expresses Christophe's intuitions of the divinity. In the agonizing transition from life to death, he imagines himself struggling with a divine orchestra, trying to extract the musical resolution of an enigmatic, precariously balanced discord dictated to him by some mysterious source. Christophe feels himself carried, impotent, by the power of the river, not knowing where; and his intuition cannot be realized until the final moment of ascent to the Spirit, when he rejoins the ocean-source of his stream of being. At the same instant he understands the key to the harmony which has eluded him. He is ready to embrace death and with it the totality of being which life has concealed from him; to submerge himself in the eternity which his previous creative ecstasies permitted him only to glimpse; and to *be* in everything, as music, as eternity, as God, resolving all contrasts in the final seizure of death. At the same time, true to his commitment to the creatural, physical aspect of death, Rolland interweaves with this spiritual description a parallel observation of corporeal dying. Christophe's efforts to unravel the mystery which confronts him, to emerge from the limited consciousness which life imposes on him, are reflected in the moments when the narrator disengages himself from the stream of Christophe's wandering consciousness. At times, this observation is through the eyes of the character himself as he regains consciousness. In these moments his sensation of existence in the external world is imperfect, already obscured by the half-completed process of submersion. He is not sure to what extent his agonies are really perceptible outside himself.

The response, when it comes, is not from without, but from the "invisible orchestra" which his spirit is trying to dominate (pp. 1589 ff.). These spiritual struggles on the deathbed are reflected in, or perhaps emanate from, the movements of his body in its death throes. Christophe sits up painfully in his bed to be seen better by the instrumentalists. He waves his arms feverishly about in order to set the rhythm. He cries out in his enthusiasm over this heavenly orchestra's perfect rendition of the difficult music he has created— a fulfillment of all his past promise. He curses his body for its insufficiency to deal with the demands of the task, and it takes revenge by a fit of coughing which drowns out the music. He wrestles with this body which refuses to loose its hold on his spirit for the final ascent and at last succeeds in wrenching himself free from its grip. He sheds tears of happiness, which the young girl tending him (into whose consciousness the reader is momentarily submerged) reverently wipes away. The last effort of his body coincides with his final attempt to see the object of his journey, the flowing of the river over its banks, inundating the plain and rejoining the sea. This farewell to his corporeal self is not, it can be seen, a felicitous passing into the realm of the spirit. The last struggle, by the importance it gives to the material aspect of the death throes, acknowledges the claims of the body on the soul, the formidable nature of this fraternal enemy which, in its refusal to admit defeat, defines the role which the life and death of the body play in Rolland's conception of the musician's creative act.

The interaction of the predominant metaphors in this climactic passage of *Jean-Christophe* with the physical description of the hero's death indicates clearly the inseparability of Rolland's life-metaphors—the river and the mountain road—from the creation of music. Christophe's life itself is, in a certain sense, a metaphor of the musical process and architecture, or else Rolland's conception of both life and art are functions of the dominant musical motifs which inform the novel. The identification of the hero's transition from the world to death with the resolution of a dissonance into harmony is Rolland's final definition of life in metaphysical terms. It seems safe to say that, in the context of the novel at least, metaphysics and music are fused into a symbolic whole.

There is, however, another, nonmetaphysical aspect of music which runs in counterpoint to this dominant theme examined in this chapter and the preceding one. The understanding of the nature of music and the musician in *Jean-Christophe* would be incomplete without examining the external, social function of music in the world of men. Rolland's treatment of the subject, which runs throughout the novel, emerges as the dominant theme in the central volumes, from *La Foire sur la Place* to *Les Amies,* and is perhaps best represented metaphorically by the title *Dans la Maison.*

III. THE COMPOSER IN THE WORLD
OF MEN

The "Eclair de Tolstoï"

Some of the deepest contradictions in Rolland's thought on music appear in his works dealing with the social role of the arts. Our examination of Rolland's ideas on the nature of music and the musician's participation in his internal world and the external world of all-being or Becoming has shown that he viewed music as an emanation of the nature of things imposed upon the consciousness of the musical creator. It does not exist for a purpose: it simply exists. The composer's intuition of the universe's substance and structure dictates his inspiration. The process of composing is thus an act of discovery rather than an act of invention. Of course, the mark of a great composer, one who like Christophe has "become classic" through his increasing awareness of the shape of this universe, is his rational mastery over the material dictated by inspiration. This power, however, reflects an inherent order of the universe from which music emanates, rather than one imposed on artistic creation to make it coincide with political, social, or aesthetic preconceptions. Rolland finally rejects the term "art for art's sake" because of dilettante connotations, but in fact the structure of his musical aesthetic rests on the premise that music exists by its own internal necessity, without essential reference to external causes or purposes.

The reader is further led to this assumption by Rolland's notes from one of his earliest creative periods, 1890, when he was working on the still undefined project of the "roman de Beethoven." He had already written his first Renaissance dramas, *Orsino* and *Les Baglioni*. Certain pages of his diary contain an idea of the creative process as it operated in himself, which foreshadows his conception of this process in the great composers:

Ce qui me soutient malgré moi, c'est une vitalité enragée, qui veut réaliser l'être intérieur. Je ne vis qu'à condition de *créer ma vie,*—de créer la vie, que je ne trouve pas autour de moi,—que je ne trouve pas comme je veux, même chez les plus grands hommes, chez les artistes préférés . . . . Je dois mourir ou créer. La création artistique n'est pas pour moi une carrière ou un plaisir, c'est une nécessité de vie ou de mort.[1]

This stage in the development of his artistic individualism into the heroic ideal of *Jean-Christophe* is early evidence that the process of artistic creation represented for Rolland a necessity stronger and more real than the artist's commitment to the world of men.

The enduring quality of this sentiment is shown by its recurrence in the author's writings. It is implicit in Rolland's judgment on the morality of the artist, as can be seen in a letter to Sofia Bertolini in 1903:

Tout en admettant que Schumann a été sûrement plus moral, au sens ordinaire du mot, que Wagner, je vous dirai que je n'en juge pas moins Wagner infiniment supérieur, même moralement . . . . La moralité du génie n'est pas tout à fait la même que la moralité bourgeoise. . . . Une âme à la Wagner est une sorte d'âme de condottiere grandiose, enfermée dans le monde de l'art.[2]

In his approval of the morality of the *Übermensch,* Rolland apparently proclaims the separation of the artist from the world by virtue of his genius. Since he knew well the circumstances of Wagner's life, this endorsement of the composer's special moral status seems to include not only his unique love-life, but his social habits—the avoidance of obligations, the unashamed sponging—and his abdications of political belief, the disavowal of the revolution of 1848, and the ambiguous vassalage to Ludwig II of Bavaria. This emphasis on the internal world of the artist remained an important part of Rolland's thought up to the period of the First World War. Indeed, by judicious selection of texts from *Jean-Christophe,* one

1. Published in "Le Grain de Vie," p. 204.
2. *Chère Sofia, I,* 136.

might prove the overwhelmingly Nietzschean character of the hero and reinforce the argument with evidence from Rolland's personal writings.

Nevertheless, a dissonant strain of humanitarianism runs through Rolland's works from the beginning, at times concurrent with the opposing theme, at times in alternation. It often seems to overwhelm the internal ideal of artistic creation to the point of denying the individual's creative liberty. As early as the *Credo quia verum,* Rolland indicates his awareness of the conflict between these two ideas in himself by his desire to reconcile "smiling serenity, ironic peace: Plato, Goethe, Renan," "the ardor of passion (Italian Renaissance)," and "Tolstoy's charity." [3] With the broadening of his intellectual and artistic experience, the alignment and wording of these conflicting ideals change. The first two elements are joined under the heading of heroic individualism, in opposition to the third. But basically the problem which Rolland envisaged at the age of twenty-two remained with him into his maturity—a dialogue of the author with himself in which first one, then the other voice drowns out its rival. These are not merely complementary aspects of a given problem: in Rolland's presentation of these two conceptions of musical creation, the reader often senses a mutual logical and ideological exclusion, the conflict of opposing forces in one artistic personality. One of the grandest aims of *Jean-Christophe* is the ultimate reconciliation of these conflicting elements.

It is impossible, of course, to attach such a profound sentiment as Rolland's humanitarian impulse to a single influence. Certainly he was endowed with a temperament, a sensitive introspection, which made him aware of humanity's collective needs as well as the desires of the creative hero. Rolland's knowledge of pain, reinforced by his long experience with illness, made him deeply sympathetic with those whose lives were spent in intimate contact with hunger, disease, poverty, and spiritual disenfranchisement. This is true, certainly, of many artists and intellectuals, but few have shown such an active commitment in life and art to the cause of humanitarianism as Rolland did during the long course of his public career. His Nobel prize in 1915 was but one recognition of this fact.

3. *Cloître,* pp. 374–75.

Nevertheless, the specific conflict between individualistic and socially oriented art which is of concern here can be connected to a surprising degree, from Rolland's earliest period until the completion of *Jean-Christophe,* to the influence of Leo Tolstoy. Like the interplay of the two basic artistic concepts, this influence takes the form of a continuing dialogue, whose vicissitudes reflect the dialectical pattern so typical of Rolland's intellectual progress. Almost from its initial appearance in the experience which Rolland called the "éclair de Tolstoy," the Russian writer's influence tended to express itself as a metaphor of individualism and solidarity which gradually became the symbolic "house" of *Dans la Maison.*

"L'éclair de Tolstoy" came somewhat after that of Spinoza—shortly before Rolland's entry into the Ecole Normale. As described in *Le Voyage intérieur,* it was a less immediately literary experience than was his intuition of the world substance while reading the *Ethics.* The revelation of Tolstoy was preceded by a personal experience which Rolland's readings seemed to underline later as if by coincidence. The experience somewhat resembled the "éclair de Spinoza," giving him a sensation of liberation from prison in a physical and spiritual sense. During a trip in the North, Rolland's train stopped abruptly in the middle of a tunnel. The lights went out, and the passengers, their anxiety reinforced by the memory of a recent accident, waited for the worst. Rolland himself was at first overwhelmed by this common fear, but as he turned over in his mind the emotions and circumstances in which he was involved, fear was succeeded by a vision of freedom, of indestructibility: "Et ce fut comme si le tunnel s'ouvrait. Je voyais, audessus, les champs dans le soleil, les luzernes ondulantes, les alouettes qui montaient." [4] He had an intuition of his solidarity with all existing, living things and no longer felt threatened by anything which might happen to his individual physical person, because the revelation showed him his survival in these other forms which would continue to exist and to be generated after him:

> Non! l'on ne me tient pas. Plus fluide que l'air, Protée aux mille formes, je glisse entre les doigts, je m'échappe au travers

---

4. *Le Voyage intérieur,* p. 56.

des planches et des ferrailles tordues, et des chairs écrasées, et des voûtes de pierre. Je suis ici et là, partout, et je suis tout.[5]

This vision might be taken as a reinforcement, with different imagery, of the Spinozan revelation. The terms are more concrete, less metaphysical, but the tendency is much the same, an enlargement of the individual experience of life through an intuition of extra-human continuity. About a year later, however, Rolland reinterpreted one facet of his experience in the light of his first reading of *War and Peace*. Again, as with Spinoza, it was a particular passage which brought about the transformation: he was struck by the parallel between his own experience and Pierre Bezukhov's during his imprisonment by the French. Pierre also is "liberated" from his body by a sensation of omnipresence in nature which comes upon him one night. The terms in which his revelation is described are very close to Rolland's (it is of course possible that Rolland, transcribing his experience years later, enhanced the similarity):

> La pleine lune était arrivée au zénith. Les bois et les champs se dessinaient alentour; et au delà de ces champs et de ces bois inondés de lumière l'oeil se perdait dans les profondeurs d'un horizon sans limites. Pierre plongea son regard dans le firmament nocturne.—'Et tout cela est à moi, pensait-il, tout cela est en moi, tout cela c'est moi! . . . Et c'est *cela* qu'ils ont pris, c'est *cela* qu'ils ont enfermé dans une baraque!' [6]

An element latent in Rolland's original description of his experience, which the passage in *War and Peace* brought out as if by photographic development, is the role of Rolland's fellow passengers in his revelation. Tolstoy concludes his description of Pierre's ecstasy by having him return to the group of comrades from whom he has wandered and go to sleep peacefully among them. This acquired sense of participation in the life of all the world serves as a bond between him and his fellowmen: the existence which he

5. Ibid.
6. Ibid., p. 57.

leads individually is reflected in theirs, and they are united in a common freedom, despite their imprisonment, by virtue of this expansion of the individual into all of creation. When Rolland summarized the experience in the tunnel as it appeared to him following his first reading of Tolstoy, kinship with humanity emerged as the dominant element, rising above the theme of his liberty:

> C'est avec le même sourire [that of Pierre returning to his comrades] que j'ai, depuis le jour du tunnel, fait le voyage de la vie, plus d'une fois traversant la nuit interminable de tunnels pleins de menaces, et couché dans le troupeau de mes compagnons hommes. Et je sentais leur sueur, le frémissement de leur chair; et ma chair frémissait, comme la leur, de passions contraires, de désir, de dégoût, de douleur, de colère, et de peur.—Mais j'étais *'les champs et les bois inondés de lumière,'* et les alouettes qui montent vers le ciel, et la paix.[7]

It is curious, however, how little space Rolland devotes in his *Voyage intérieur* to the "éclair de Tolstoy" compared with the "éclair de Spinoza" or with Malwida von Meysenbug, for instance, especially taking into account the frequent and enthusiastic references to Tolstoy in his Ecole Normale diary. Between his first contact with Tolstoy and the writing of *Voyage intérieur,* Rolland's intellectual and spiritual relationship with the Russian author underwent many modifications. The impression one receives from the numerous references to Tolstoy in his diary during the years at the Ecole Normale is that of a youthful passion. Rolland's creative talent was of course not yet sufficiently formed to speak of an influence beyond the level of enthusiasm. It is nonetheless apparent, in terms of the aspects of Tolstoy's thought which left the greatest mark on Rolland's later writings, that Rolland's idea of Tolstoy at that time was not entirely relevant to the latter's real influence. There is some injustice in Rolland's claim, in his notes to the diary from 1912 (only a year after the publication of his *Vie de Tolstoï*), that this youthful period was "sans doute l'époque de ma vie, où j'ai le plus senti

7. Ibid.

son influence, et où son esprit a le plus agi sur le mien." [8] The biographical tribute to Tolstoy which he had just written [9] indicates a more deeply felt debt than the effusions of his student days.

Rolland tried to elude this paradox and to explain away, in *Le Voyage intérieur,* the appearance of filial devotion which the *Vie de Tolstoï* gives:

> J'ai contribué moi-même à égarer l'opinion, parce que, dans ma piété filiale envers le cher génie, j'ai, dans le petit livre écrit au lendemain de sa mort, instinctivement écarté tout ce qui nous séparait et voulu seulement déposer sur sa tombe mon hommage d'amour. [10]

It is true that, at this time, Rolland's obedience to Tolstoyan socioaesthetic doctrine was in the process of transition toward a more radical view of the artist's relationship to society. In his movement toward Marxism following the war, Rolland left Tolstoy behind under the influence of the catastrophic changes which his prophetic vision had long foreseen. But there is a long intervening period, which Rolland's memoirs seem to ignore, when Tolstoy's influence is felt powerfully in his writing.

It is Tolstoy the artist who exerted the greatest attraction for Rolland in the beginning: *War and Peace* was the touchstone against which every literary effort had to be assayed. He praised *Madame Bovary* because its "wonderful realism" made it "le seul roman français que je puisse opposer à Tolstoy, pour l'impression profonde de vie, de vie totale." [11] Tolstoy's panoramic vision of the passions and movements of the multitudes seemed the most valid concern of the novel, but his epic quality appeared to be beyond the capacities of the French. In later years, Rolland admitted the importance of this aspect of Tolstoy's art as a model for *Jean-Christophe.* [12]

8. *Cloître,* p. 155.
9. *Vie de Tolstoï,* first published in the *Revue de Paris* (Feb. 15, Mar. 1 and 15, Apr. 1, 1911).
10. *Voyage intérieur,* p. 54.
11. *Cloître,* p. 6.
12. *Voyage intérieur,* p. 52.

Although Rolland later denied the intellectual influence of Tolstoy and claimed that even in the beginning he found his thought "gourde et flasque,"[13] Tolstoy figured strongly in the composition of the *Credo quia verum;* his appeal to Rolland lay not only in their spiritual kinship but in the structure of his thought. During the first term at the Ecole Normale, Rolland called Tolstoy one of his four "beloved thinkers": the other three were Spinoza, Wagner, and Renan. He cited the following passage from *War and Peace* as one of the basic elements of his "doctrine":

> Tout ce qui vit, est Dieu . . . . Globe animé, frémissant, sans contours nettement indiqués, dont la surface se compose de gouttes d'eau serrées en masse compacte, qui glissent en tous sens . . . c'est l'image de la vie . . . . Dieu est au milieu. Chacune de ces gouttes essaie de s'étendre pour mieux le refléter. Elle grandit, se resserre, disparaît, pour revenir de nouveau à la surface.[14]

Rolland felt a similar sense of identification with the other works of Tolstoy he read: *The Death of Ivan Ilyitch, The Power of Darkness,* and *Scenes of Sebastopol.* During his "practice teaching" at the Lycée Louis-le-Grand, he read passages from these works to his classes.[15]

When, in the final formulation of the *Credo quia verum* of 1888, Rolland wished to strike a balance between art and humanitarianism, he expressed it in terms which are Tolstoyan, in contradiction to Platonic-Renanian irony:

> Sans doute, je ne crois à l'existence humaine qu'à la façon dont je crois aux rôles qui s'agitent sur un génial théâtre. Il est donc naturel que j'aime les vivants, comme j'aime Hamlet ou Ysolde; je n'ai pas mille façons d'aimer. Seulement, il y a entre les divines créations de l'esprit humain (l'art) et les divines créations de la chair, cette différence que les dernières participent au drame dont je suis acteur, et que j'ai mille occasions vivantes de

13. Ibid., p. 53.
14. *Cloître,* p. 89.
15. Ibid., p. 291.

manifester pour elles mon amour, qui reste purement idéal pour les oeuvres d'art. De celles-ci le monde ressemble au mien, il en est le reflet transfiguré, mais il n'est pas le mien; je ne puis pas y entrer, agir, et *me sacrifier.*

Car la suprême vérité dans nos rapports de vie avec les êtres qui nous entourent, c'est le *Sacrifice.*[16]

Although there is no essential difference between the natures of real and fictional roles, the former are the only ones which permit one to arrive at that annihilation of the illusory self sought by Rolland's Spinozism. The work of art can be at best a symbolic sacrifice, and its exaltation of the individual self into all-being must remain an idea, not a fact.

Although he placed Tolstoyan charity at the head of his list of virtues, Rolland's attitude toward the thought of his avowed master was already tinged by doubt. The point of contention lay precisely in the relationship between the aesthetic and the ethical. During early summer of 1887, after reading the recently published *What Are We To Do?*, Rolland wrote a letter to Tolstoy expressing his dilemma: how to reconcile his admiration for the author with his equally deep love of art, which Tolstoy tended increasingly to condemn? Almost fifteen years later, when he published the long letter Tolstoy sent in reply, he described the state of mind which Tolstoy's denigration of art had created in him at that time:

J'aimais profondément—comme je n'ai jamais cessé d'aimer—Tolstoy. Depuis deux ou trois ans je vivais enveloppé de l'atmosphère de sa pensée; j'étais certainement plus familier avec ses créations, avec *la Guerre et la Paix, Anna Karénine,* et *la Mort d'Ivan Illiitch,* qu'avec aucune des grandes oeuvres françaises. La bonté, l'intelligence, l'absolue vérité de ce grand homme, en faisaient pour moi le guide le plus sûr dans l'anarchie morale de notre temps.

Mais, d'autre part, j'aimais l'art avec passion; depuis l'enfance, je me nourrissais d'art, surtout de musique; je n'aurais pu m'en passer; je puis dire que la musique me semblait un aliment

16. Ibid., p. 374.

aussi indispensable à ma vie que le pain.—Aussi, combien fus-je troublé, en lisant chez celui que j'étais habitué à respecter et à croire, ces violentes invectives contre l'immoralité de l'art! [17]

In September 1887, Rolland wrote a second letter to Tolstoy, asking him notably if he really found satisfaction in the abandonment of thought for manual labor, as he proposed. The question's importance is indicated by Rolland's appeal: "J'ai besoin de conseils. Autour de moi, nul directeur moral. Des indifférents, des sceptiques, des dilettantes." [18] Five years later, in a similar period of moral torment, Rolland recalled this appeal to Tolstoy and the effect of the latter's reply:

> Je traversais encore cette douloureuse crise morale, au bout de laquelle je pressentais la lumière, mais bien lointaine, bien faible, et je cherchais autour de moi qui m'aiderait à m'en approcher. Je cherchai partout, je ne trouvai qu'un coeur, d'une infinie bonté, qui ne pouvait rien pour moi; c'était le cher Tolstoy, du fond de sa Moscovie.[19]

Tolstoy's reply reached Rolland in October of 1887, and he and Suarès read the letter together. Tolstoy dealt with two of the basic questions which Rolland posed: what is the nature of "real" art, and what is the relationship between the artist and society? Tolstoy's definition of art is the same in this letter as that which he proposed a decade later in *What Is Art?*. It is, as would be expected, essentially a moral, not an aesthetic, definition, and one which accords with the current of his thinking in later years, although the tone of the letter is less dogmatic than in his last works. His argument rests on the identity of the Beautiful and the Good, defined as the physical and spiritual well-being of man:

> Le bien et le beau est défini depuis des siècles. Les Brahmanes, les sages des Bouddhistes, les sages des Chinois, des Hébreux, des Egyptiens, les stoïciens grecs l'ont défini, et l'Evangile l'a défini de la manière la plus précise:

17. *Une Lettre inédite de Tolstoï*, p. 8.
18. *Cloître*, p. 157.
19. *Choix de lettres à Malwida von Meysenbug*, p. 64 (Mar. 1892).

> *Tout ce qui réunit les hommes est le bien et le beau,—tout ce qui les sépare est le mal et le laid.*
>
> Tout le monde connaît cette formule. Elle est écrite dans notre coeur.[20]

This definition of art implies Tolstoy's response to the second question: the relationship of the artist with society. True art can exist, under these terms, only for the sake of the betterment and the union of men; there can be no question of "art for art's sake," because the product of any such aesthetic, according to Tolstoy, is not art. Since the artist shares the burden of all men of good will, his primary concern must be for undertaking his responsibility, not exploiting others, not living in leisure while others are forced to toil. In addition, physical labor is the most rewarding and the most natural form of human activity.

> Planter un arbre, élever un veau, nettoyer un puits—sont des actions indubitablement utiles aux autres et qui ne peuvent ne pas être préférées par un homme sincère aux occupations douteuses qui, dans notre monde, sont prêchées comme la vocation la plus haute et la plus noble de l'homme.[21]

What would be the fate of art if all artists were required to take up a manual trade? Would it not exhaust the artist and prevent him from giving his creative energies over to the enduring products of art? In Tolstoy's view, a trade would be salutary to any real artist and disabling only to artistic parasites. The extra energy and fervor required for mere participation in art after a day's work would be proof of the artist's sincere vocation and would guarantee the validity of his creative efforts:

> Le travail manuel est un devoir et un bonheur pour tous; l'activité intellectuelle est une activité exceptionnelle, qui ne devient un devoir et un bonheur que pour ceux qui ont cette vocation. La vocation ne peut être connue et prouvée que par

20. *Une Lettre inédite de Tolstoï*, p. 25.
21. Ibid., p. 20.

le sacrifice que fait le savant ou l'artiste de son repos et de son bien-être pour suivre sa vocation. Un homme qui continue à remplir son devoir: celui de soutenir sa vie par le travail de ses mains, et, malgré cela prend sur les heures de son repos et de son sommeil pour penser et produire dans la sphère intellectuelle, fait preuve de sa vocation.[22]

As in *What Is Art?*, Tolstoy devotes as much space in his letter to the exposure of "false" art as he does to the definition of true art. In his view, the degeneracy, uselessness, and isolation of contemporary art were due to the fact that the artists of his time, unlike those of the past, formed a separate and privileged caste, claiming intellectual superiority over the masses rather than aiming at their pleasure and edification. As a result of the creation of this caste and its erection of "false" art as an ideal, the foundations of European culture have been sapped. The artist is in a difficult position: he must choose between the obvious material advantages of an artistic career and the difficulty of a life of labor and sacrifice, exempt from the "superstitions" of contemporary culture (which Tolstoy likens to the superstitions of established religion):

Ce qu'on appelle dans notre monde les sciences et les arts ne sont qu'un immense *humbug,* une grande superstition dans laquelle nous tombons ordinairement dès que nous nous affranchissons de la vieille superstition de l'Eglise. Pour voir clair la route que nous devons suivre, il faut commencer par le commencement,—il faut relever le capuchon qui me tient chaud, mais qui me couvre la vue. La tentation est grande. Nous naissons,—ou bien par le travail, ou plutôt par une certaine adresse intellectuelle, nous nous hissons sur les marches de l'échelle, et nous nous trouvons parmi les privilégiés, les prêtres de la civilisation, de la *Kultur,* comme disent les Allemands; et il faut, comme pour un prêtre brahmane ou catholique, beaucoup de sincérité et un grand amour du vrai et du bien pour mettre en doute les principes qui vous donnent cette position

22. Ibid., p. 22.

> avantageuse. Mais pour un homme sérieux qui, comme vous, se pose la question de la vie,—il n'y a pas de choix.[23]

Despite Rolland's gratitude, the views expressed in Tolstoy's letter do not seem for the moment to have had any positive influence on his ideas concerning art. The letter marks a landmark in Rolland's esteem for Tolstoy the humanitarian; nonetheless, from this time, he had less consideration for Tolstoy as a theorist of art. It was not until the turn of the century that the two facets of his esteem again converged on the same level. Tolstoy's decline in Rolland's opinion can be felt almost immediately in his diary and correspondence after the letter's arrival:

> Même Tolstoy m'abandonne. C'est-à-dire que je l'abandonne. C'est un homme comme les autres. Et sa réforme de l'art est une réédition de celle de Rousseau, plus sincère, et faite par une nature qui y était mieux préparée. Les préoccupations morales l'emportent trop, chez lui, sur les préoccupations artistiques.[24]

A year later, he wrote to his mother from Rome: "Tolstoï a tout compris, sauf l'Art." [25]

The *Kreutzer Sonata* only increased Rolland's reaction against Tolstoy's ideas on art. He found in it what he expected: a condemnation of music on moral grounds which served more to underline Tolstoy's intellectual weaknesses than to shake Rolland's faith in the greatness and moral quality of the art itself:

> Le titre m'avait bien fait supposer que Tolstoy essaierait d'y montrer l'influence morale ou démoralisatrice exercée par la musique sur des âmes, et en particulier sur des âmes faibles, des âmes de femmes. Moi-même, c'est un sujet que j'ai traité autrefois, et que je poursuivrai plus tard. Mais Tolstoy était tout à fait incapable d'en faire le fond de tout un roman, par la bonne

23. Ibid., p. 27. This is one of the few passages in the letter where Tolstoy injects a personal note, and where one senses that this is a dialogue between an old sage and a young seeker of guidance, rather than the moralizing monologue of a great old man communing with his paper.

24. *Cloître*, p. 187 (Feb. 1888).

25. *Printemps Romain*, p. 67.

raison qu'il n'est point musicien, et très peu artiste (ce qui ne l'empêche pas d'être un génie).[26]

Still, Rolland felt Tolstoy's denunciation of music on moral grounds to be strong enough to justify a response in his doctoral thesis:

> Ce sont de terribles puissances qu'ils ont [composers] entre les mains; en elles-mêmes elles ne sont ni bonnes, ni mauvaises; à vrai dire, elles sont bonnes toujours, puisque ce sont des forces pour l'action, mauvaises seulement par l'usage qu'on en fait.
>
> J'ajouterai que le drame musical, à certains égards plus factice, moins véritablement humain que la musique pure, a moins de dangers qu'elle. Dans le plus violent de ses romans, Tolstoy a montré quels ravages pouvaient faire dans les âmes médiocres les sublimes passions du plus noble des musiciens. Ces forces obscures et ignorées, ce déchaînement de fureurs, où le génie se délivre de ses souffrances, jetteront le trouble dont il s'est soulagé, son désordre maladif, dans les coeurs effarés, mal faits pour le comprendre. Elles ne feront de bien qu'aux âmes de sa taille, qui reconnaîtront en elles les angoisses dont elles souffrent, et dont elles ne pouvaient se délivrer.[27]

It is surprising that the publication in France of Tolstoy's *What Is Art?* did not alienate Rolland further on the question of art. Its denunciation of modern literature, painting, and music should have been repugnant to Rolland, with his exalted view of creative activity. Among the chief targets of Tolstoy's moral wrath were Beethoven and Wagner, and yet Rolland's reaction to excerpts from the text was surprisingly mild, even sympathetic. In a letter to Malwida von Meysenbug in February 1898, he wrote: "Il est malheureux qu'il compromette *une si belle cause* par des jugements aussi légers et incomplets. Les décadents auront beau jeu." [28] Any conflict in his mind seems to be with Tolstoy's means of proving his points rather than with his object.

In *What Is Art?*, Tolstoy enlarges on some of the ideas sketched

26. Ibid., p. 309.
27. *Origines du théâtre lyrique*, pp. 13–14.
28. *Choix de lettres à Malwida von Meysenbug*, p. 225 (italics mine).

in his letter of 1887 to Rolland, developing more fully his concept of aesthetics, his definition of art, and his attack on the cultural elite of contemporary Europe. Tolstoy's weapons are those of the pamphleteer: he carefully excludes anything that would weaken his case. He pretends to give objective descriptions of the works he is analyzing but presents absurd condensations to make them seem grotesque. He refuses to admit the good faith of those he attacks and makes liberal use of the technique of guilt by association. For a moral reformer, he manifests an extraordinary amount of bad faith, as when he judges three volumes of poetry "objectively" by turning to page 28 of each. Emerging from this egregious example of bias, the theme of artistic reform and the ideal of a union of mankind through art succeed in giving the book a certain nobility and profundity. Following his denunciation of contemporary art, Tolstoy outlines an "art of the future" quite different from Wagner's, an art of tenderness and humanity:

> The art of the future will thus be completely distinct, both in subject-matter and in form, from what is now called art. The only subject-matter of the art of the future will be either feelings drawing men toward union, or such as already unite them; and the forms of art will be such as will be open to every one. And therefore, the ideal of excellence in the future will not be the exclusiveness of feeling, accessible only to some, but, on the contrary, its universality. And not bulkiness, obscurity, and complexity of form, as is now esteemed, but, on the contrary, brevity, clearness, and simplicity of expression. Only when art has attained to that, will art neither divert nor deprave men as it does now, calling on them to expend their best strength on it, but be what it should be, a vehicle wherewith to transmit religious, Christian perception from the realm of reason and intellect into that of feeling, and really drawing people in actual life nearer to that perfection and unity indicated to them by their religious perception.[29]

If Rolland took a more conciliatory attitude toward this reiteration of ideas already expressed in Tolstoy's letter, it was due in great

29. *What Is Art?*, p. 173.

part to the events in his life and the changes in his political and social views which have been mentioned previously. The Dreyfus affair brought him into increasing contact with socialist circles, as did the public reaction to his play *Les Loups*.[30] Although Rolland was disturbed by the distorted interpretation of the play seized on by both the Dreyfusards and their opponents, it seems to have established him as a proponent of the former camp and identified him with the socialists: Péguy published the work in their first collaboration; a year later, Jaurès made a speech of introduction at the premiere of Rolland's *Danton*.

Publication of "Une Lettre inédite de Tolstoï"

From this time on, Rolland's acceptance of Tolstoy's ideas on art paralleled his association with Charles Péguy; the most Tolstoyan expressions of Rolland's aesthetic were published in Péguy's *Cahiers de la Quinzaine*. Rolland's preface to the *Lettre inédite de Tolstoï*,[31] his first contribution to the *Cahiers*, shows almost complete acceptance of Tolstoy's doctrine. *Le Théâtre du peuple*, the following year,[32] is an adaptation of Tolstoy's basic artistic premises to a Western, more industrialized society. Both of these works have strong implications for music, although their primary areas of interest are, respectively, art and theater.

I do not consider justifiable Leo Schrade's claim that Rolland created the heroic Beethoven of his biography almost entirely as a result of his association with Péguy.[33] Rolland's mixed reaction to the Dreyfus affair has already been indicated, and his unsteady association with Péguy never took on the aspect of a master-disciple relationship. But association with Péguy, along with collaboration in the *Revue d'art dramatique,* involved Rolland in the movement which called forth his most Tolstoyan writings: the popular theater. Rolland's introduction to Tolstoy's letter contains statements about the relationship between art and the people which foreshadow the

30. Presented in May of 1898 by Lugné-Poë's *Théâtre de l'oeuvre,* under the title of *Morituri* and the pen-name "Saint-Just."

31. *Cahiers de la Quinzaine,* Ser. 3, No. 9 (Feb. 1902).

32. Ibid., Ser. 5, No. 5 (Nov. 1903).

33. In *Beethoven in France,* Schrade insists that this Beethoven was a "Beethoven of Dreyfusism" and reflected Péguy's own socialist vision more than the "aesthetic" vision of Rolland himself.

doctrine of *Le Théâtre du peuple* and show his debt to Tolstoy. He agrees here with Tolstoy that real art cannot be created without a public, not of the elite, but of "un peuple qui ait un coeur sain, une intelligence saine, un regard sain, qui sache voir, sentir, comprendre tout ce qu'il y a de beau et de bon dans le monde, et qui travaille à en orner la vie.[34] For that audience, and not the elite for whom art existed in his time, Rolland sees a new kind of artist who will steep himself in the life of the people, sharing their labor instead of using his gift as an escape:

> Il ne me déplairait pas, je l'avoue, qu'on pût obliger les artistes à rentrer dans la condition commune, qu'on parvînt à répartir entre tous les hommes sans exception la somme de travail manuel, nécessaire à soutenir et à entretenir l'édifice social. Partagée entre tous, elle ne serait pas assez écrasante pour empêcher les vrais artistes de faire leur art par surcroît; mais elle suffirait à enlever aux faux artistes tout désir de prendre sur leurs heures de loisir pour se livrer à une occupation intellectuelle.[35]

Rolland's diminishing esteem for Richard Wagner at this time can be ascribed in great part to the influence of Tolstoy. In an early letter to Sofia Bertolini, Rolland indicates the opposition in his mind between the two and his growing preference for Tolstoy, of whom he says: "Je le regarde comme le seul homme vraiment grand aujourd'hui, (plus grand même que Wagner: du moins je le préfère)."[36] This change in valuation was based largely on the question of aesthetics and social purpose: in a letter dated soon after, Rolland stated that Wagner's vision of art was invalidated by the egoism which lay at its base:

> Bayreuth ne fût-il pas tombé dans la niaiserie d'une religion de famille, il était dès le principe le produit exclusif du génie égoïste de Wagner. Quelle faiblesse suppose chez un grand homme cette unique recherche du triomphe pour sa personne et pour ses oeuvres! Quelle joie peut-il bien goûter à cette domi-

---

34. *Lettre inédite de Tolstoï*, p. 10.
35. Ibid.
36. *Chère Sofia*, *1*, 12 (Aug. 1901).

nation purement matérielle sur des troupeaux d'hommes sans liens communs, sans pensées communes, réunis seulement par les caprices de la mode et d'aveugles sensations! Le premier souhait et devoir d'un homme de génie ne devrait-il pas être de former autour de lui un peuple d'hommes libres, intelligents, fraternisant dans l'amour et la recherche de la vérité? [37]

Le Théâtre du peuple

Attracted to the popular theater movement which flourished around the turn of the century in the militant socialist atmosphere fostered by the Dreyfus case, Rolland witnessed the efforts of one of the first groups, Maurice Pottecher's *Théâtre du peuple,* to re-establish the links between art and the masses. During the summer of 1897, he attended outdoor performances of two plays given at Bussang, in the Vosges, by Pottecher, whose family owned a factory in the area. Rolland was struck by the thirst for art of the crowds who attended these presentations in pouring rain and wrote to Malwida von Meysenbug:

J'aurais voulu que vous ayez pu voir surtout les répétitions du soir, quand parfois il pleuvait à torrents, et que le peuple assis dans la prairie autour, restait silencieusement, des heures sans bouger, sans parler. Ces pauvres gens! y a-t-il assez longtemps qu'on les avait privés de nourriture spirituelle! [38]

He sent glowing articles to *Le Temps* and the *Journal des Débats,* in which, as he admitted to Malwida, he exaggerated his praise, "car il faut à tout prix qu'une oeuvre pareille réussisse. J'y vois un fait d'une importance sociale de premier ordre, une révolution dans l'art."

In 1899, Rolland took part in efforts organized by the *Revue d'art dramatique* to promote the establishment of a congress of European popular theaters during the Universal Exposition of 1900. An *Enquête sur le théâtre populaire* was published in the *Revue d'art dramatique* in November of that year; that same month, Rolland

---

37. Ibid., p. 20 (Sept. 1901).
38. *Choix de lettres à Malwida von Meysenbug,* p. 210 (Aug. 1897).

was a co-signer, with such literary figures as Anatole France, Robert de Flers, Octave Mirbeau, and Zola, of a petition to the Minister of Education seeking government support for the program.

Rolland's concern for an artistic medium to satisfy the needs of the masses extended itself naturally to the field of music. His hand is evident in one item of the *Revue d'art dramatique* survey: "Le théâtre populaire sera-t-il uniquement littéraire,—ou faut-il faire une place à la musique, soit sous forme de drame lyrique, soit sous forme de concerts?"[39] The question presented itself in two forms: the selection and promotion of works of the past which reflect the interest of the people and the creation of authentic expressions of their contemporary life.

In *Le Théâtre du peuple,* Rolland discusses the suitability of great music—the music which has achieved greatness in an elite tradition—for popular art. In the context of the moral and aesthetic criteria which this manifesto proposes, the author's previous judgments are modified. Rolland finds very little music from the past which would fit the needs of a contemporary mass public (his discovery of Handel had hardly begun at this date), and the two figures who dominated his tastes from his youth until this time, Wagner and Beethoven, are not excepted from his exclusion.

We have already noted Rolland's opposition of Wagner to Tolstoy, which the Russian author himself made abundantly clear in *What Is Art?*. Since Rolland was seeking principally the qualities of healthiness and joy for the encouragement of the people, all of his work except portions of *Die Meistersinger* seemed excluded from a popular repertory: "Quel profit le peuple pourrait-il tirer des complications maladives de cette sensibilité, de la métaphysique du Walhalla, du Désir de Tristan qui souffle la mort, et des tourments mystico-charnels des chevaliers du Graal?"[40] Rolland was concerned lest the masses be contaminated by bourgeois taste rather than find artistic expression of their own.

Beethoven, whose life Rolland had just offered as a heroic model in the *Cahiers,* is also judged unsuitable for a mass audience. The

39. Cited in *Théâtre du peuple*, p. 191.
40. Ibid., pp. 48–49.

people Rolland's biography aimed at were an oppressed minority, a cultural and moral elite: "ceux qui ne se résignent pas à la médiocrité de l'âme."[41] It was a group with which Rolland identified closely, but not the public aimed at by the popular theater movement. For this audience Beethoven's music was too personal, too much a reflection of his struggles and emotions, and, in its highest manifestations, too inaccessible. Rolland called instead for a new music which, like Tolstoy's "art of the future," would speak to and for the majority of mankind, uniting huge audiences in feelings of joy, hope, and brotherhood. He defines the qualities of this music quite clearly in his manifesto.

More than any other part of the treatise, the section dealing with scenic disposition reflects music's role in popular theater. Rolland does not treat this so much from the point of view of music's physical presence in the theater, although he discusses that briefly, relegating music to a secondary role. Rather, musical ideas, musical thinking, are fundamental to his outline of what popular theater must be. One might expect Rolland's idea of dramatic construction to bear the same relationship to music as his conception of the novel: that is, the emanation of its form from the flow of its internal Becoming, the reflection in literary structure of the laws of being and therefore of music in its metaphysical sense. But how far Rolland was, at the time of *Le Théâtre du peuple,* from this concern with individual intuition of the universe is indicated by its total absence from this work. His usual concern for essences was not entirely displaced but found its expression in a different kind of temporal reference and medium. Rather than sound in depth the time-stream contemporary with his own life, Rolland turned toward that aspect of the stream which captured Péguy's imagination: the racial, historical flow of Becoming manifested in a people.

The genre which Rolland considered particularly adapted to the needs of his contemporary public in France was the historical epic or pageant. His ideas on the production of this kind of spectacle were inspired to a great extent by an eighteenth-century musician, Grétry. Rolland found in Grétry's *Essais sur la musique* an outline

41. *Beethoven,* p. 3.

which almost flawlessly suited the idea he was forming. It was not
Grétry's musical production which satisfied Rolland's criteria:
Grétry's ideas on his art, published in the *Essais,* were separated by
a wide margin from his realization of them. But Grétry in his
later years had an intuition of the potential role of music and art
among the people, which reflects not only his experience as member
of the *Institut national de France,* inspector of the *Conservatoire,*
and favored citizen-composer during the Revolution, but also what
Rolland called "a conception of happiness which foreshadows Tolstoy's," citing from the *Essais* the following passage:

> Les plus sages d'entre les hommes voient enfin que c'est en
> faisant des sacrifices aux autres que nous méritons qu'ils en
> fassent pour nous.—Mais, de cette manière, nous ne vivons donc
> que de sacrifices?—Oui.—C'est donc là le bonheur général?—Il
> n'en est point d'autre.[42]

Grétry's "curious sketch for a new theater"[43] presents the case
for a kind of musical drama on a monumental scale, suitable for the
populace of the new nation, and designed both to please and to
elevate the taste of the public. He proscribes the devices of aristocratic art which are no longer valid for the new era:

> Dès qu'il s'agit d'intrigues amoureuses, de pièces d'intrigues
> proprement dites, de sujets champêtres ou familiers, ce n'est que
> par mille détails, par les *a parte,* par mille jeux de physionomie,
> que les acteurs peuvent présenter des vérités de ce genre; ce
> n'est que par mille nuances entre le fort et le doux, par mille
> agréments, petites notes, trilles, batteries, *pizzicato, arpeggio,*
> que le musicien compositeur peut rendre la vérité des détails
> moraux qui constituent une action non exagérée; et tous ces
> petits moyens, si précieux dans un cadre ordinaire, sont nuls
> dans une grande salle.[44]

42. Cited in *Musiciens d'autrefois*, p. 264.
43. *Théâtre du peuple*, p. 111.
44. Ibid.

Grétry proposes some essentials for establishing a large-scale musical theater, which agree strikingly with Rolland's experience in the popular theater:

> Voici ce qu'il faut observer: 1° que le poète ne traite que des sujets historiques déjà connus; alors la plus courte exposition suffira; 2° qu'il ne présente que des masses, de grands tableaux ornés de pompe, marches, sacrifices, combats, danses, pantomimes toujours rapides lorsque ces objets ne sont qu'accessoires de l'action principale; 3° que tous les morceaux de poésie destinés au chant mesuré soient simples, et ne renferment qu'un sentiment . . . . De là naîtra l'énergie, la rapidité, la variété que demande un tel spectacle.[45]

He deals most comprehensively with techniques for creating a lyric art suitable for mass audiences in a great auditorium—broad, spacious melodies ("Le musicien ne travaillera qu'*en grosses notes*"), simple, slowly changing harmonies, freedom from excessive detail in the orchestration, exclusion of technical subtleties in the harmonies and in the melodic line, syllabic setting of the text ("presque toujours note et parole"), in everything breadth at the expense of detail and precision: "C'est un tableau fait pour être vu à une grande distance; c'est alors qu'il faut en quelque sorte peindre avec un balai." [46]

It is interesting to note how closely Grétry's recommendations match those of Tolstoy, who criticizes the excessive subtleties of contemporary "French-inspired" art and proposes a return to the subjects and forms which have pleased the greatest number for the greatest period:

> The form of the art of the future will . . . not be inferior to the present forms of art, but infinitely superior to them. Superior, not in the sense of having a refined and complex technique, but in the sense of the capacity briefly, simply, and

45. Ibid., p. 112.
46. Ibid.

clearly to transmit, without any superfluities, the feeling which the artist has experienced and wishes to transmit.[47]

Both Tolstoy and Grétry were indebted, of course, to the ideas of Jean-Jacques Rousseau in this domain. Rolland's early tendency to view the latter as a less sincere and less responsible predecessor of Tolstoy gave way, in his maturity, to an admiration which he expresses in his introduction to *Les Pages immortelles de J.-J. Rousseau*.[48] But Rousseau's intransigent ideas on the theater and his plan for collective *Fêtes du Peuple* seemed far too advanced and too divorced from contemporary reality to be of relevance to Rolland's practical aims in *Le Théâtre du peuple*. It is interesting to remember that Rolland later returns to the eighteenth century for an idea of music's role in the popular theater. Handel, however, provided him with a model of his aims realized in concrete terms, not simply with the theoretical, ideological basis for popular art.

Let us note in passing, before leaving the subject of Rolland's manifesto, that the final period of *Jean-Christophe,* which sees the hero transcending his hopes for a popular, "objective" art form, corresponds roughly in time with the second edition of *Le Théâtre du peuple;* in his introduction to the manifesto Rolland refers to it as a "historical document," full of "youthful flaws," which reflects an ideal that cannot be fullfilled in France, "une vieille terre, dont le peuple s'est laissé peu à peu conquérir par les classes bourgeoises, pénétrer par leurs pensées, et n'a pas de désir plus vif que de leur ressembler." [49]

It is not surprising to find that a great deal of material from *Le Théâtre du peuple* appears in *Jean-Christophe.* Since Rolland tended to crystallize his ideas around certain rhetorical, synthetic formulas, the reader often happens upon a sentence for the third or fourth time, uncertain as to the exact location of the previous encounter. These encounters are made more disconcerting by the fact that, on occasion, the same formula is made to serve different

47. *What Is Art?,* pp. 171-72.
48. Paris, 1938; cf. *Cloître,* p. 187; *Printemps Romain,* p. 311.
49. *Le Théâtre du peuple,* nouvelle édition (Paris, 1913), p. 3.

ends in different contexts. As his opinion or frame of reference changes, Rolland frequently keeps the same descriptions, the same epithets, varying only the surrounding or concluding material in order to bring the expression up to date with the evolving stream of his ideas. This tendency can be illustrated by the changing portrait of Richard Strauss in Rolland's articles on Germany, music reviews, correspondence, and diary and by Strauss' representation in the character and through the eyes of Jean-Christophe (since he is at once a reflection and a fictional contemporary of Strauss).

The Tolstoyan elements in the musical ideas of *Jean-Christophe* are also affected by this rule. Not only does the musical ideology of the hero express itself in themes which alternate and to a certain extent combat each other, as each strives for dominance in the novel, but each of these themes tends to develop within itself according to the same law of change, with the result that, from the first volume of the novel to its conclusion, a complete metamorphosis takes place. For this reason I do not feel it justifiable to call *Jean-Christophe* a Tolstoyan novel, as it has been characterized by some critics. Take as an example a recent tribute to Rolland in a literary journal:

> Le plus fidèle disciple de Léon Tolstoï en France fut incontestablement Romain Rolland. La correspondance échangée entre les deux écrivains en témoigne, et il n'est pas douteux que *Jean-Christophe* corresponde exactement à la définition de l'artiste telle que nous la rencontrons dans *Qu'est-ce que l'art?* [50]

Even without the word "exactement," this judgment is untenable. The novel ranges over too wide a spectrum of viewpoints, and its hero embodies too many conflicting tendencies. But Tolstoyan themes do play a vital part in the novel's development, and, although they frequently are negated or disappear for a while, they constantly reemerge in the personality of the hero-musician and perform an essential function in his artistic progression.

There are three basic Tolstoyan themes in the novel: the popular

---

50. Guy Bayard, "Tolstoï et la France," *Les Nouvelles littéraires* (Dec. 15, 1960), p. 9.

sources of "real" art; the humanitarian, charitable aims of "real" art; and the implied converse of these two ideas—the majority of what passes for art, according to the contemporary European definition, is "false" art, the product of corruption or of weakness. The growth and development of these intertwining themes give rise gradually, in the context of the novel, to the metaphor of the "house" in *Dans la Maison*. The Parisian *immeuble* in which Christophe lives, surrounded by isolated representatives of the moral strength of France, is the symbolic medium through which Rolland can explore the racial and historical heritage of the nation, combat the reigning "false" art which grips Parisian cultural life, and promote an ideal of unity and spiritual elevation on a national scale. The house is also, by the ineluctable law of movement underlying *Jean-Christophe,* an ideal to be transcended and negated by a succeeding vision of universal unity which breaks its walls. As was seen in Rolland's account of his Spinozan revelation, walls exist to be broken and therefore perform a necessary function in the author's vision of liberty.

Tolstoy and the Folk Sources of Music in Jean-Christophe

The theme of music's folk sources makes its first appearance in the novel near the end of *L'Aube* (p.88). One may justly infer from its rather late entry into Christophe's artistic experience that this element is not a primal source of Christophe's musical creativity. It acts more as a control on existing tendencies, a check against the dangers of individualism and of virtuosity as an end in itself. Indeed, that is essentially the role which this theme continues to play throughout the novel.

Christophe's uncle Gottfried is the human embodiment of the force of folk inspiration in the development of Christophe's artistic personality. Symbolically, Gottfried is the brother of Louisa, Christophe's mother. In Christophe's genealogy his father's family, the Kraffts, represents his purely musical talent: the paternal generations of musicians have never realized their potential but foreshadow Christophe as the generations of Bachs prefigure Johann Sebastian. The maternal side represents up to this point a peasant stock upon which the Kraffts look condescendingly. Christophe's father Mel-chior, wasteful and destructive of his talent, married beneath his station, taking a girl of no education or particular beauty. Louisa is tolerated and perhaps grudgingly respected for her goodness and patience by Christophe's grandfather, Jean-Michel. Until her brother's appearance in the novel, however, this strain of peasant virtue plays only an incidental role in Christophe's formation. As a result, the young Christophe tends to share his paternal family's con-descension toward his mother.

Gottfried's entry into Christophe's life changes this attitude in the young hero. His uncle is a mysterious wanderer who alternately gives impressions of profound intuitions and of simple obtuseness. He has several virtues which could be called Tolstoyan: a deep re-ligious sentiment, an unresisting acceptance of his situation and of the annoyances which the world inflicts upon him, an unperverted simplicity, and an incapacity to lay claim to cultural values which the Kraffts' prestige has imposed upon his sister. He arrives at a crucial point, just after Christophe's first imitative compositions, ac-claimed by his grandfather as tokens of future glory, have almost succeeded in going to the young boy's head. Christophe has learned how to set down series of notes which recall the music of respected writers of the past. He is honest and intelligent enough to sense dimly that one must have something to say before writing.

> Mais la peine qu'il se donnait pour savoir ce qu'il pensait, et pour le fixer par écrit, faisait qu'il ne pensait plus rien, sinon qu'il voulait penser quelque chose. Il ne s'en obstinait pas moins à construire des phrases musicales; et comme il était naturelle-ment musicien, il y arrivait tant bien que mal, encore qu'elles ne signifiassent rien. (p. 87)

The endorsement given to these imitations by his grandfather would be enough to save him from the pangs of conscience and self-analysis, except for Gottfried, who reveals to him not only the dangers of this approach to musical creation but an antidote to sterility in popular themes. It is not by any means the only solution, but Christophe will repeatedly return to it during his life.

The scene in which Christophe's eyes are opened to his uncle's vision contains the familiar elements of other revelations in *Jean-Christophe*: night is falling; Christophe and Gottfried are seated on the grass; mist is rising from the Rhine before them. Here, for one of the first times, Christophe is in the presence of the symbolic agents of his life-stream. In the rays of the setting sun, Gottfried's ugly face takes on a sad dignity which stills the banter Christophe has been preparing. As darkness falls, amid the sounds of the crickets and the lapping of the river's waters, Gottfried unexpectedly begins to sing. His song is childish, grave, monotonous: "Elle semblait venir de très loin, et allait on ne sait où. Sa sérénité était pleine de trouble; et, sous sa paix apparente, dormait une angoisse séculaire" (pp. 90–91). Christophe is astonished and deeply moved. Gottfried is unable to tell him what the song is, who wrote it, or how old it is. All he knows is that it exists and is as necessary to the moment as the sounds of nature; another such song, despite Christophe's pleas, would be superfluous. To Gottfried, music must be an instinctive expression of man's emotions at a given time. In Christophe's previous experience, music has been made for its own sake, because there was time and opportunity. By that definition, Gottfried insists that what he has sung is not music. It was not made; it has always existed. Why make music, he asks Christophe, when songs already exist to meet every need? Any music that goes beyond these needs, created out of the mere desire to create or to obtain renown, is incomprehensible to Gottfried. What reason can there be for a musician to be a "great man"? His nephew can only answer lamely, "in order to write beautiful music" (p. 92).

Tolstoy devotes considerable space in *What Is Art?* to this point. The necessity of music to the moment of its performance is a basic criterion of his critical judgment. He finds this aptness of artistic expression to circumstances, emotions, or moods exemplified by the music of the Russian peasants and contrasts such "natural" music with music of the salon:

A few days ago I was returning home from a walk feeling depressed, as occurs sometimes. On nearing the house I heard the loud singing of a large choir of peasant women. They were welcoming my daughter, celebrating her return home after her marriage. In this singing, with its cries and clanging of scythes, such a definite feeling of joy, cheerfulness, and energy was expressed, that, without noticing how it infected me, I continued my way toward the house in a better mood, and reached home smiling, and quite in good spirits.[51]

When, during the same evening, a guest plays a work of Beethoven's later period (the piano sonata Opus 101), Tolstoy senses not the need to transmit feeling, but the desire to make a work of art. When Tolstoy calls this to the attention of the other guests, who also heard the peasants' earlier music, his opinion is received with amused contempt.

Tolstoy does not claim that all classical or serious music is unworthy of consideration as art. He excepts "the melodies of Bach (his arias), Haydn, Mozart, Chopin, (when his melodies are not overloaded with complications and ornamentation), and of Beethoven himself in his earlier period." [52] But he does not give them privileged status because of their place in the cultural tradition. Rather, it is despite their acceptance by connoisseurs that he is willing to grant them equality with folk songs. It is the "pleasant, clear, and strong musical impressions which are transmitted" by the music of the established composers which give them their value, and not their technical mastery, formal complexity or regularity, or alleged profundity of emotion.

It is according to this reasoning that Gottfried judges Christophe's first attempts at musical creation. The scene in which Christophe submits his music for his uncle's consideration, a few days after the revelation of Gottfried's kind of art, presents this implied converse of the question. Not only is Gottfried in possession of a worthy kind of art, but he calls Christophe's works false. Christophe's principal object in composing was the satisfaction of his vanity: "Tu as été orgueilleux, tu as menti: tu as été puni . . . . Voilà! On est

51. *What Is Art?*, p. 127.
52. Ibid., pp. 127–28.

toujours puni, lorsqu'on est orgueilleux et qu'on ment, en musique. La musique veut être modeste et sincère" (pp. 95–96). He has merely imitated the established composers in what seemed to him an "original" way. Despite his unwillingness to see the truth of his uncle's charges, Christophe is forced to admit them to himself.

Gottfried's criticism and Christophe's acknowledgment of it represent a dual victory for Tolstoy's ideas and a defeat for the Kraffts' respectable enlightenment. Christophe's ineradicable contact with the popular wellsprings represented by Gottfried marks the first step in a new direction. For the first time, he is capable of regarding his paternal heritage with objectivity, seeing an alternative course of action, and controlling his progress toward realization of his musical gift by reference to the real source of creation.

Gottfried's victory has another significant implication. It represents the affirmation of one of Tolstoy's central ideas: that the artist's communion with the source of his inspiration is essentially a religious act. Tolstoy made the assertion of this belief as unequivocal and dogmatic as possible: "If a religious perception exists amongst us, then our art should be appraised on the basis of that religious perception." [53] His definition of the "religious perception of our time" is, as might be expected, a specialized one. It is "the consciousness that our well-being, both material and spiritual, individual and collective, temporal and eternal, lies in the growth of brotherhood among all men." [54] In this respect, the perception represented by Gottfried differs from Tolstoy's. But Gottfried, like the author of *What Is Art?*, expresses his musical criticism in religious terms. Christophe's first attempts at writing not only are futile; they are offensive to God, the source of real creation: "Qu'est-ce qu'elle est [this music]? Une impiété, un blasphème contre le Seigneur, qui nous a fait présent du beau chant pour dire des choses vraies et honnêtes" (p. 96). Music must be created outdoors, played and sung in the fields or on the road, because that is where we can feel the spirit of God unencumbered in His "cher petit air frais." There is no contradiction of Tolstoy's religious ideas in this particular form of artistic and religious perception, but Gottfried, like

53. Ibid., p. 138.
54. Ibid., p. 139.

Tolstoy's peasants, is closer to the sources, less capable of universalizing what he feels into social dicta.

One question poses itself here: why should the peasant be more capable of producing what Tolstoy calls art than the enlightened members of a social and cultural elite? What prevents one of the upper class from having the same perceptions and expressing his feelings with the same validity as a peasant or a peddler? Tolstoy's view is unequivocal. The most important "condition of contagiousness in art"—the primary factor in communication between artist and audience—is sincerity.[55] The man who most possesses that quality will be most able to produce works of art. The peasant does not know the shibboleths of culture or pretend to greater erudition than he possesses. He can see no reason to give his creations a complicated form. He is not really creating for an audience, but for himself and others like him. And he is in constant direct contact with nature and the primary emotions, which evolve out of the struggle for a livelihood, the joys of productivity and usefulness. Tolstoy claims, without qualification, that sincerity "is always complied with in peasant art, and this explains why such art always acts so powerfully; but it is a condition almost entirely absent from our upper-class art, which is continually produced by artists actuated by personal aims of covetousness or vanity."[56]

The peasant, like the child, is too devoid of intellectual vanity, too close to the sources of art, to think of producing imitative art. This same directness and simplicity protect him from being taken in by the false art purveyed in the great cities of the West. Tolstoy professed to have received letters from peasants indignant at the raising of a statue to Pushkin in Moscow and too unsophisticated to understand how "a man of more than easy morals, who was killed in a duel," and who wrote "often very indecent poetry about love," could receive the honor due to "a holy man and teacher of goodness."

A similar perplexity must trouble the brain of a Breton or Norman peasant who hears that a monument, "une statue"

55. Ibid., p. 134.
56. Ibid.

(as to the Madonna), is being erected to Baudelaire, and reads, or is told, what the contents of his "Fleurs du Mal" are; or, more amazing still, to Verlaine, when he learns the story of that man's wretched, vicious life, and reads his verses.[57]

Rolland's peasants in *Jean-Christophe* are not as simple or as idealized as Tolstoy's. They are more earthy and sensual—partly, perhaps, because Rolland is dealing not with the Russian peasantry Tolstoy knew so exclusively, but with a German version which the French author visualized mainly as a fictional embodiment of the milieu and atmosphere in which folk art comes into being. Their personification of the "earth-spirit" gives them a less moralistic tone. Christophe's experience of the peasant's direct relation to nature, with the ambiguous sensuality of those who live from the earth, is initiated by the sight of a peasant girl working in the fields, whose animal vitality stirs in him an impulse toward rape and murder. The pent-up sexual force of his adolescence is the motor in this incident, but the physical attraction emanating from the peasant girl is the key to its unleashing. Far from sharing the Tolstoyan peasants' alleged unconcern with sensual love, Rolland's radiate sensuality and indulge in a heavy, explicit gallantry.

This sensuality lies at the roots of the peasants' communion with nature and gives rise to their folk music, even more strongly than their "innate spirituality." As the Tolstoyan peasant is more sincere in his artistic creation because of his preoccupation with essential things, Rolland's tiller of the soil has a parallel superiority over the city-dweller. But the precise definition of these essential things is different, and the difference reflects the spiritual inclinations of the two authors. Paradoxically, it is the ascetic, physically delicate Rolland who vaunts the luxuriant earth-spirit of the peasants, while the robust Tolstoy glorifies their abstinence and sobriety. The two writers, however, share a common attitude toward these seemingly opposed traits: both see them as symptomatic of healthiness and sincerity. Rolland's peasants cannot help singing when the mood and the occasion call for it, as when, in *L'Adolescent,* drifting down

57. Ibid., p. 158.

the river in small boats, they spontaneously burst into four-part harmony, as natural and necessary to the scene as the trees of the fields (p. 295).

Tolstoyan "Charity" in Jean-Christophe

The seeds of Christophe's artistic involvement in the popular sources of music are planted a considerable time before his realization of the need for art to be directed back at the people. Gottfried's revelation of unsuspected expressive resources in anonymous popular culture has the nature of a mystical experience, a specific direction given to the quest for communion with the life-source. It is a much traveled route by which Christophe's artistic individuality can penetrate the mysteries which his sensibilities have previously suggested to him. The implications of this need to enter into communication with the neglected masses go at first only in one direction—toward the artist, who absorbs material as a creative nourishment with no obligation to repay the debt thus incurred. The question that runs through the series of volumes preceding Christophe's departure from his homeland is that of validity of inspiration. When the audience comes into question, it is in a negative manner: Christophe is the victim of a public unable, because of insincerity or prejudice, to give his genius the response it deserves.

In *L'Aube,* Christophe's public is the court of his provincial Rhenish town. There can be no question of its being a real sounding board for the young musician's creative gifts. The court audience exists not because of any real need for musical satisfaction, but because it is traditional in Germany, even in the smallest capitals, for the arts to be furthered. The audience is an artificial one in terms of music's internal necessity. If Christophe is still too young to be able to realize consciously how unsatisfactory, and indeed unnecessary, this audience is, he can nevertheless sense its lack of qualification to judge him and its insincerity. This is brought home to him when, immersed in a performance of Beethoven's *Coriolan* overture which precedes his debut, he is startled to hear the music come to a halt in mid-measure and give way to the national hymn, signaling the prince's entrance: "Le passage d'une musique à l'autre était si brutal et si inattendu, que Christophe en grinça des dents, et tapa du pied avec colère, montrant le poing au mur" (p. 102). The irrelevance of the praise which follows Christophe's performance, culminating in official recognition of his status as "Hofmusicus," serves only to increase his separation from his public.

In the succeeding volumes of *Jean-Christophe,* the hero's native city seems to grow in size and complexity with his increasing awareness and maturity, as a result of Rolland's narration from the point of view of his protagonist. In parallel fashion, Christophe's public expands: the ducal concert hall gives way to the opera house and *Städtische Tonhalle,* the court audience to a larger public of connoisseurs and culture-minded bourgeois. Christophe takes his place, thanks to the favor of the court and the prestige of his family, among the professional musicians of the city. But he cannot find a sounding board for his ideas and innovations. The stolid burghers are interested in paying tribute to the traditions of German art through audition of the old works or of imitative new ones. Christophe grows increasingly impatient with their Philistinism in *La Révolte.* Since he feels it necessary to be sincere, the tension grows stronger until finally, deprived of his noble protection by a temperamental outburst, Christophe finds himself also deprived of the last vestiges of tolerance by his wider public. Immediately after his dismissal by the grand duke, he is subjected to public humiliation by the local orchestral society, now free to avenge insults which Christophe unwisely heaped upon Brahms (p. 505).

Through the succeeding volumes, it is implied that the composer, although he must draw part of his inspiration, basic vocabulary, and style from the common fund of folk culture, is isolated by his gift from all save a select, pitifully small public. The possibility of Christophe's reaching even a limited group of appreciators is negligible. It is only by a freak of chance that Christophe discovers the effect of some of his published works on a man in another town. This instance, one of the rare examples during Christophe's youth in Germany of the artist's successful communication, is doubly apt: the works in question, a volume of *lieder,* represent his effort to make use of the pious folk sources first revealed to him by Gottfried.

In *L'Enlisement,* shortly after the public catastrophe referred to above, Christophe decides to consecrate his isolation and reaffirm his artistic integrity by publishing at his own expense a collection of some thirty *lieder,* "de ceux qui lui plaisaient le plus, et, par conséquent, qui plaisaient le moins au public." These are some of his most characteristic works, those which appeal less on the basis of melodic facility than on the basis of aptness to text, fidelity to the sentiment and meaning of the poem. This is, of course, a reminiscence of Hugo Wolf, whose career Christophe reflects strongly during this phase. The texts qualify as popular material on the basis of their spirit, their age, and their place of origin. Paul Gerhardt, the author of one of the lyrics reproduced in Rolland's text, is described as "a naïve, pious poet," whose piety and reflection of provincial spirit qualify him as a folk poet for Christophe and Rolland:

> L'optimisme souriant du pieux Paul Gerhardt charmait aussi Christophe. . . . Il aimait cette vision innocente de la nature en Dieu, les prairies fraîches, où les cigognes se promènent gravement au milieu des tulipes et des narcisses blancs, au bord des ruisselets qui chantent sur le sable, l'air transparent où passent les hirondelles aux grandes ailes et le vol des colombes, la gaieté d'un rayon de soleil qui déchire la pluie, et le ciel lumineux qui rit entre les nuées, et la sérénité majestueuse du soir, le repos des forêts, des troupeaux, des villes et des champs. (pp. 511–12)

The inspiration of this *Chant d'été,* if too sensual for Tolstoy's ideal, nevertheless corresponds to Gottfried's vision of nature, as does Gerhardt's *Lied du Voyageur chrétien.* Of course, Christophe's settings of these lyrics, by their individuality and passion, reflect the spirit of this period of his life. His genius is still too egotistical, too subjective, to permit a literal translation of these works into music: they are transformed into post-romantic *lieder* along the lines of Wolf's works or Mahler's songs with orchestra, emphasizing the passional, arrogant presence of the artist in nature: "Le vieux Gerhardt eût frémi de l'orgueil diabolique que respiraient maintenant certaines strophes de son *Lied du Voyageur chrétien,* ou de l'allégresse païenne qui faisait déborder comme un torrent le flot paisible de son Chant d'été" (pp. 511–12). But this is the result of Christophe's isolation and the emphasis it places on his own artistic personality rather than on the popular source of the lyrics. Indeed, there is no outlet for these creations: the published volumes, in accordance with Christophe's desire, remain unpublicized and unsold.

These works, described in *L'Enlisement* as zealously kept in the publisher's store, contrive somehow to reach the attention of Peter Schulz, a retired professor of musicology living in another town. One of the most moving chapters of *La Délivrance* describes the old man's receipt of the volume, among a packet of the "dernières nouveautés" sent to· him by his bookdealer (p. 555). It is Christophe's setting of the *Christliches Wanderlied* which lifts Schulz from the depression into which he has fallen. Schulz knows the words well already, but Christophe's musical setting sheds new light on them, revealing to him a younger, more vigorous spirit which nonetheless corresponds and communes with his own across time and space. For the first time in *Jean-Christophe,* the possibility of direct, purely musical communication between hero and audience is raised. What takes place is the annihilation of barriers between creator and receptor. By the meeting of souls in the highest form of musical communication, in a perfect relationship of artist and audience, Christophe and Schulz share the experience of artistic creation.

Christophe's face-to-face encounter with old Schulz, one of the emotional climaxes of the novel, is arranged by Rolland as part of the alternating pattern which informs his hero's life. It comes immediately after Christophe's visit with Hassler, a successful composer: Christophe finds Schulz on the rebound, as it were, from this frustrating meeting. After a long train journey undertaken with the express purpose of seeking encouragement from this older colleague whom he had met some years before, Christophe is greeted with indifference, irony, and scorn. Hassler has been soured and morally exhausted by his long struggle to arrive, and success has completed the process of disintegration in him. (Here again, in Christophe's fruitless interview with Hassler, whose cynicism is enhanced by his recognition of Christophe's talent, can be seen reminiscences of Hugo Wolf and his similar experience with Wagner.[58]

Rolland takes pains to juxtapose these examples of professional incomprehension and amateur enlightenment and to unite them by his use of parallelism and antithesis. Long journeys precede the two meetings: one begun in hope and anticipation but culminating in profound dejection; the other, the return, begun in despair but ending in an unexpected emotional fulfillment. The gap between generations is an abyss in the first case but is bridged by Christophe's music in the second. Hassler's premature senility, which strikes Christophe when he first sees him, is counterbalanced by Schulz' hearty open-mindedness in old age. The sense of abject solitude which the encounter with Hassler leaves in the hero contrasts with the powerful sense of human solidarity which he feels at the end of his stay with Schulz. The element of chance, of fortuitous event, is a powerful binding theme running through both episodes: Christophe happens upon Hassler in a particularly negative mood, the latter's belated note of conciliation arriving too late to stop Christophe's departure; Christophe notices by chance the name of Schulz' town on a railway timetable, and the two men miss each other at the station and almost do not meet. But finally, Christophe does find Schulz, and they return to the latter's house, where the composer at last has the opportunity to share his musical creation with a receptive and enlightened audience.

Rolland makes it clear at this point, as he will elsewhere, that this is a more essential relationship than that between composer and performer. Certainly the community of feeling between Christophe and Schulz is far more immediate than that between the composer and Pottpetschmidt, Schulz' friend who sings Christophe's *lieder*. It is true that Christophe finds in him a surprising penetration of their meaning, all the more astonishing when this musical gift is compared with the unprepossessing appearance of the singer. Rolland takes pains to insist on this incongruity, which is remi-

58. See *Musiciens d'Aujourd'hui.*

niscent of similar passages elsewhere. The recreation of musical experience, which for Rolland is an essentially internal phenomenon,
does not depend on the physical qualities of the artist. Indeed, this
ideal communion in music seems not to depend even on the physical
quality of the sound which serves as its medium: this is implied in
the case of Christophe's friend Emmanuel, whose painful voice is
an obstacle to the musician, until he learns to "hear the music, and
not the instrument" (p. 1492). But there is no doubt that in Rolland's evaluation of the relative importance of composer, performer,
and listener, the middle figure occupies the lowest rank. To under-
score his point, Rolland has Pottpetschmidt indicate the irrelevance
of his own individuality to musical communication—indeed, its
destructive effect. As soon as the singer realizes his success with
the composer, he begins to assert his personality, to interpret the
music, and undoes the good which he has accomplished.

Only Schulz, the gentle and infirm old man, is possessed of
sufficient character for the generous abandonment of self required
of Christophe's ideal appreciator. The entire personalities of the two
men enter into this highest form of musical experience. Indeed,
Schulz has his energies sapped almost to the point of collapse by
its powerful demands. Along with his spiritual exaltation, upon
Christophe's departure he is overcome by a physical lassitude which
serves as an index of the degree to which communion in music has
involved his entire being.

The effect on Christophe of this extended moment of contact outside of himself is quite different. Part of the reason lies, of course,
in the external differences between the two men: age, temperament,
and physical resources. More than that, however, the difference is
explained by the nature of the activities each man has engaged in.
For Schulz, the experience is an invasion by an outside force, which
takes possession of his spirit and manipulates it. The impact of
Christophe's music is like that of a drug which raises the barriers
preventing absolute depletion of the body's resources. At the same
time it provides a foreign energy which the old man does not himself possess, using him as if he were capable of matching the capacities which produce it. These are to some extent foreign to and

greater than Christophe himself, emanating from nature, transmitted to him in the process of inspiration. Once Schulz is deprived
of these external sources of strength and their artificial stimulation,
he is left shattered by overexertion.

For Christophe, however, this release of energies within himself
is a necessary purgation. The outlets of his creative energy have one
by one been stopped up, so that he could not even set himself
putative, potential releases for what he continued to store up in
himself as a kind of psychological safety valve. He has recently
failed in his attempt to receive encouragement from Hassler; this
was preceded by the tragic end of his love affair with Sabine, the
closing-off of intellectual and emotional contacts with his city, and
the forced conclusion of an unsatisfactory friendship with a lonely
couple, the last people in his town willing to receive him after his
open break. The death of Gottfried has eliminated his important
emotional and aesthetic contact with an outside entity:

> La dernière amitié virile et sereine, qui eût été capable de
> soutenir Christophe, s'était engloutie dans le gouffre. Il restait
> seul, avec sa mère vieillie et indifférente à sa pensée,—qui ne
> pouvait que l'aimer, qui ne le comprenait pas. Autour de lui,
> l'immense plaine allemande, l'océan morne. A chaque effort
> pour en sortir, il s'enfonçait davantage. La ville ennemie le
> regardait se noyer. (p. 537)

In contrast with this "enlisement," Christophe's mood after his
stay with Schulz is one of expansion. Rolland describes him as "ras-
séréné . . . rendu plus confiant en soi par l'affection qu'il laissait
derrière lui" (p. 582). He is refreshed, capable of welcoming the
creative spirit into himself. For the first time, the reader is made
conscious of the coming of spring, the season traditional to the expansion of creative genius and henceforth adopted by the author
in his cycle of musical creation. Christophe repeatedly will respond
to the rebirth of nature with renewed activity. The Alpine springtime which brings about his creative renascence in *Le Buisson
ardent,* when the *foehn* takes possession of him, is the most familiar
example of this. But Schulz' existence and Christophe's acknowledg-

ment of it are a necessary impulsion to the composer's acceptance of the natural phenomenon. Rolland emphasizes the significance of this catalytic presence by introducing, in rapid succession, two themes interwoven with that of human emotional contact: that of Gottfried and that of Christophe's search for a satisfactory public.

Reference has already been made in the preceding chapter to Christophe's discovery of the house in which Gottfried died, an episode which succeeds the musician's departure from his friend Schulz' house. This juxtaposition of narrative elements serves to make the reader conscious of Gottfried's role as personification of the German folk spirit, the peculiar idealism underlying German thought, and Christophe's sense of isolation and dissatisfaction in the context of the German spiritual and musical tradition. Neither Schulz nor the blind girl, Modesta, can suffice to reconcile Christophe with his country or to provide him with the intelligent audience which the composer requires.

At the close of the first great division of *Jean-Christophe*, which presents the hero's life in Germany up to the moment of exile, Christophe is in a state of almost total separation from his public. The act of departure from his native soil represents a search for a people in whose name and whose behalf he may create. Rolland, reflecting his earlier articles, complains that the German people, since the victory of 1871, have lost even the nobility of blind idealism.[59] Coexistent with a humanitarian renunciation, the product of years of political submission, he finds a delight in force and a respect for might at the expense of disinterested right, which seems to be the obverse of their submissive optimism. What Christophe needs is something hard and resistant against which to exert his talent and his energy. The German people are too capable of absorbing anything in the way of nourishment for the soul and body. In their gluttony, they do not distinguish between Beethoven and Brahms, between Mozart and Auber. Christophe's reaction is against the soil, the native spirit of his Germany. It leads him away from the geographic definition of his country toward France, away from the ethnic, popularly oriented search of his years of adolescence and

59. Ibid., pp. 175–96.

young manhood toward an intellectual, rather than a spiritual, center: the Paris of his imagination, magnet of German intellectual migrations:

> En lisant les volumes de Herder et de Fichte, que le vieux Schulz lui avait légués, il y retrouvait des âmes comme la sienne,—non *"des fils de la terre,"* servilement attachés à la glèbe, mais des *"esprits, fils du soleil,"* qui se tournent invinciblement vers la lumière.
>
> . . . Christophe, comme tant d'autres grands musiciens allemands dans la détresse, se tournait vers Paris. (pp. 598–99)

The search for a world with which to wrestle in the struggle to create and communicate leads him for a time to hope for satisfaction from an intellectual elite, as source and charitable goal of his creative gift, until the moment of deception turns him back toward a different soil.

Music and Society in Jean-Christophe

The violent criticism to which Romain Rolland has been subjected, on patriotic grounds, since the publication of *Jean-Christophe* is well-known. Before the First World War, he was called un-French, anti-French, Germanic, and pro-German in his sympathies and art. In spite of the attack on German cultural life in *La Révolte,* his choice of a German rather than a French musical hero gave rise to a reaction which was given further fuel by publication of *La Foire sur la Place,* with its satire of the musical milieus of Paris. Too many were offended by Rolland's recognizable caricatures of contemporary musicians and critics for him to escape reprisal. In the eyes of some French critics, Rolland's alleged defection to the German side at the outbreak of the war was only the culmination of a tendency long evident in his artistic bias.[60] This, along with stylistic considerations which went against French literary tradition, accounts for a phenomenon noted early in Rolland's correspondence: the acceptance of his novel as an important literary work outside of France sooner and to a greater extent than

60. See Cheval, pp. 15–55.

in his own country. In England, for example, H. G. Wells hailed *Jean-Christophe* as the direct inspiration of a new generation of English novelists committed to social action and thought: "Notre mouvement tire ses meilleurs encouragements d'entreprises audacieuses et originales telles que celle de M. R. R. dans son *Jean-Christophe—Jean-Christophe* est le prototype de ce nouveau genre du libre roman." [61] Rolland saw himself as "chef d'école" of a group including Wells, Arnold Bennett, Joseph Conrad, John Galsworthy, and E. M. Forster. Yet evidence of even the earliest of Rolland's writings shows that he was vitally concerned with the French cultural tradition. He sought to prove its equality with the German musical heritage and to define its individuality. In his "Souvenirs de jeunesse," [62] Rolland recounts the spiritual vacuum in which he existed during his first years in Paris. Having left his native Clamecy in order to prepare for the Ecole Normale, he describes himself in the "moral whirlpool" of Paris after the defeat of 1871, unable to find his footing, restrained from falling into some undefined form of vice only by timidity and weakness. This emptiness, characterized in *Le Voyage intérieur* as a blackness into which flashed the "trois éclairs," was filled by a "jet of flame" from his "two deep gulfs of life"—nature and music.[63] It is significant that Berlioz, the only important representative of Romanticism in French music, figures as one of the two stars of Rolland's musical constellation at this crucial point. Berlioz outranks Wagner at the time and is granted a place among a "triad" in which Shakespeare is "king of kings." [64] This early partiality to a French composer is symptomatic of Rolland's musical judgments, even in the face of his commitment to the expansion of French musical taste beyond political boundaries and cultural prejudices. The consequences of this commitment to opposing points of view make themselves felt constantly in his relations

61. Cited from *Le Temps*, June 18, 1911, in a letter to Sofia Bertolini; *Chère Sofia*, 2, 113.
62. *Mémoires*, p. 21.
63. Ibid., p. 23.
64. *Le Voyage intérieur*, p. 27.

with the world of music. An early example, his exchange of letters with Camille Saint-Saëns, illustrates his resolution of an apparently irreconcilable conflict.

Saint-Saëns was one of Rolland's first minor "stars." Although by 1887, during the first term at the Ecole Normale, the original luster had worn off this music, Rolland still had sufficient consideration for Saint-Saëns to be dismayed at reports that he was part of a patriotic cabal against the presentation of Wagner's *Lohengrin* in Paris. In Rolland's letter to him can be found the common ground on which he was able to base both commitment to the French national school and "evangelism" on behalf of German musical culture. Rolland appealed to Saint-Saëns in the name of justice and pled the ability of French music to stand comparison with that of its neighbor: "Qu'avons-nous à redouter? En tout cas, rien de *Lohengrin!* Ce n'est pas une telle oeuvre qui révolutionnera notre art! Elle est trop peu différente des opéras que l'on connaît en France." [65]

Saint-Saëns' reply seemed to Rolland a signal example of bad faith and of the nationalists' secret persuasion of inferiority:

> Vous me permettrez de vous dire qu'il est profondément triste de voir la jeunesse intelligente partager si complètement les idées des gens qui travaillent à détruire l'art national et jusqu'au patriotisme lui-même, quand à nos côtés l'Allemagne et l'Italie font précisément le contraire, exaltant quand même leur pays et leur art. [66]

His reaction to this accusation was logical enough: if Saint-Saëns was afraid of penetration by an alien culture, his fear was necessarily based on a lack of confidence in the French art he claimed to be defending. Rolland later compared this accusation with those he reaped following publication of "Au-dessus de la mêlée" in 1914:

> C'est avec la même bonne foi qu'on m'a prêté, dans *Au-dessus de la Mêlée,* des sentiments anti-français, alors que, par fierté

65. *Mémoires,* p. 163.
66. Ibid., p. 164.

même de Français, j'adjurais mon pays de garder, vis-à-vis de l'adversaire, son esprit de justice et d'humanité.[67]

Rolland repeatedly demonstrates, in his writings preceding the turn of the century, his commitment to a French school of music. This is to be seen, for example, in the tribute he paid to French composers of the seventeenth and eighteenth centuries, whom he had first discovered in the library of the Ecole Normale. These inspired in him "un sentiment de respect et d'orgueil pour ma France."[68] In the operas of Lully, Campra, Destouches, and Rameau, he perceived a strong tradition leading up to Berlioz (Rolland uses the adjective "Berliozienne" in praise of Rameau). Later, under the influence of the musicologist Henry Expert, he extended the line of this tradition back to the sixteenth century, particularly to Claude le Jeune.

At about the same time, Rolland came into contact with César Franck. Franck became the first contemporary figure in music to occupy a place of importance for Rolland. From the beginning, his reactions to the Belgian composer's music were powerful, like his experience of Berlioz and Beethoven. His description of this initial contact indicates the suddenness and the profundity of Franck's effect on him:

> Jusqu'à présent [30 janvier 1887], je ne connaissais rien de lui. Maintenant, je ne puis comprendre que j'aie vécu jusqu'à vingt ans, sans m'être douté de ce qu'était César Franck . . . .
>
> J'ai été transporté par les *Béatitudes* . . . .
>
> Il y a bien longtemps que je n'avais éprouvé une aussi grande joie musicale! [69]

The *Symphony in D Minor,* heard at its premiere in 1889, came close in his esteem because of its power and originality:

> Un style d'orgue. Un développement régulier, puissant, raidi. Les phrases durement hâchées, criées par les cuivres. Parfois de

67. Ibid., p. 164n.
68. *Cloître,* p. 229.
69. *Mémoires,* pp. 166–67.

la sécheresse. Des passages brusques, sans transition, du *fff.* au *ppp.* (comme dans les *Béatitudes.*) Mais de la grandeur, de l'émotion, des pensées qui rappellent les *Béatitudes.* Une personnalité.[70]

This music seemed to express a moral uprightness, a spirituality which Rolland found extremely appealing in an irreligious age.

Rolland's writings manifest a strong sense of national pride, a desire to defend French music against its detractors and to uphold it against the indifference and scorn of the Germans. This is a dominant theme of his correspondence with Louis Gillet.[71] Gillet was at the time an instructor of French in Pomerania, and Rolland exhorted him to demonstrate the solidity of French character to German detractors:

> Ne vous lassez pas de rappeler Descartes et Balzac à ceux qui nous personnifient en Rostand et Sardou; et s'ils vous opposent la musique, demandez-leur s'ils connaissent les musiciens de nos Valois, et le *Traité d'Harmonie* de Rameau et les *Béatitudes* de César Franck.[72]

Rolland was obsessed by the German idea of French culture, the stereotype of frivolity and overrefinement fostered by political rivalry and popular prejudices. Wagner's Hans Sachs gives a typical example in his peroration of the last act of *Die Meistersinger,* contrasting loyal German art with "wälschem Dunst" and "wälschem Tand." Rolland almost seems to be playing Hans Sachs to his own countrymen in a letter of 1903:

> [The Germans] ignorent César Franck, qui est pour moi le seul génie musical depuis Wagner,—beaucoup plus pur que lui, —le plus sincère des musiciens depuis Beethoven. . . . Ils font un effort pour comprendre Berlioz; et il est pitoyable de voir comment ils le comprennent.[73]

---

70. Ibid., p. 171.
71. Ironically, Gillet broke with Rolland at the time of the war because of the latter's alleged "unpatriotism."
72. *Correspondance,* p. 101 (letter of Nov. 1900).
73. *Chère Sofia, 1,* 143.

Perhaps the best indication of the importance which French musical art had in Rolland's eyes is to be found in his answer to a survey by the musicologist Paul Landormy, "L'Etat actuel de la musique française." [74] Landormy saw fit to place it as a conclusion and summation to the question. Rolland's contribution avoids the patriotic blindness of some of his noted colleagues, while still giving just measure to the French tradition and its contemporary manifestations. He starts out with an attempt to define what the internal nature of this tradition is and what it represents in terms of the French national spirit. In doing this, Rolland foreshadows several of the issues which emerge in the middle volumes of *Jean-Christophe,* especially the relationship between French music and a French musical public. He tries to base his definition solely on the observable product of this French musical spirit in its best forms during the past centuries:

> A nous restreindre à la musique française depuis trois siècles, il me semble qu'on puisse y reconnaître comme caractéristiques (entre autres):
> 1° Des dons littéraires appliqués à la musique.
> 2° Des dons visuels appliqués à la musique: une tendance à juger la musique, du dehors, comme une architecture ou un dessin, non comme une langue psychologique, à la façon allemande.
> 3° Un certain tempérament individualiste, qui s'exprime par un goût médiocre pour le chant en commun, pour l'harmonie et, au contraire, un goût naturel et un don marqué pour la mélodie libre.[75]

Rolland's first category, literary bias, is taken from two points of view. The first is the apparent tendency of French music to "set texts," not only in operatic or lyric form, but in purely musical works based on literary pieces: tone poems or impressions. However, he refers more specifically to a second point of view, which is the justness of French musical declamation, especially the recitative. An interesting development of this point, which is only suggested in

---

74. "Réponse à l'enquête de Paul Landormy," p. 424.
75. Ibid.

the response to Landormy's questionnaire, is found in a series of letters which Rolland exchanged with Richard Strauss on the occasion
of Strauss' preparation of *Salomé* for performance at the Paris
Opéra about this time. In them Rolland champions French musical
declamation, as exemplified by Debussy's *Pelléas et Mélisande,*
against the more theatrical and distorted declamation of Wagner's
music-drama.[76]

Rolland reproaches French musicians and critics with being too
submissive to the German point of view and thus creating a pseudo-
Germanic music on their own soil. Of all the contemporary musicians, only Debussy was emancipated from the overwhelming influence of Wagner and seemed to make full use of the purely
French idiom by his concentration on the text, the plastic nature of
the melodic line, and the individualism of French melody. Debussy's
avoidance of the set piece and chorus and his use, like Berlioz, of a
light, refined harmonic structure subordinated to melody, instead of
the complex German harmonic practice, represent in Rolland's eyes
the most satisfactory contemporary French approach.

Debussy does not, however, represent for him the ideal model
for the future of French music. Indeed Rolland is troubled by the
possibility of Debussy's having too great an influence on succeeding
generations: "Le caractère excessivement raffiné de son art, d'ailleurs
très original, me fait craindre que si cette école réussissait à se
former, elle fût plutôt une école parisienne qu'une école française:
ce qui n'est pas tout à fait la même chose." [77] The central issue is
the discovery and development of a musical public whose roots
might go deeper into the soil, the history, and the spirit of the
French people than do those of the Parisian elite.

The conclusion to Rolland's response underlines the connection
between culture, national spirit, and social progress:

> J'espère donc qu'une éducation musicale plus étendue . . . et
> des conditions sociales plus favorables (plus de loisirs pour le
> peuple, une vie moins fiévreuse, plus intime, intelligente et so-

76. See *Richard Strauss et Romain Rolland,* pp. 36–81.
77. "Réponse à l'enquête," p. 425.

ciable), amèneront ce renouveau d'une nation musicale, et par suite d'une école nationale en musique. Ici comme ailleurs, les conditions sociales d'une nation sont les conditions vitales même de l'art.[78]

This is one of the principal themes of the middle volumes of *Jean-Christophe,* where the hero is engaged in the search for a French "people."

La Foire sur la Place: *Critique of the Cultural Elite*

The role played in Jean-Christophe's Becoming by *La Foire sur la Place* is a negative one. In the previous volumes, Rolland makes frequent use of the reversals of the "route en lacets qui monte" to give a fresh impulsion to his hero's progress, but he does not use it on such a large scale as an entire book. The proportions of this exposition give a just idea of its significance. Through *La Foire sur la Place,* Jean-Christophe ceases to be the hero he was in the previous volumes. Instead he becomes, during his initiation into the cultural marketplace of Paris, a polemic device of the author. Rolland uses the technique of Montesquieu's *Lettres Persanes* and Voltaire's philosophical novels: the "man from another planet," an intelligent (and ostensibly unprejudiced) outsider, who sees the follies to which natives have been blinded by habit and partisanship. Rolland's use of this device illustrates its dangers: objectivity yields to one-sided criticism, and a negative view of society's working is propounded by a character who has lost his own positive definition. This fault is all the more open to criticism in view of Rolland's pretension, in his preface to *Dans la Maison,* to be creating a man, not a novel (p. 1600). Even if that were true of *Dans la Maison* (and even there Christophe is more mouthpiece than man), it cannot be said of *La Foire sur la Place.*

This negation of the personality of Rolland's hero can only partially be justified as a function of the law of irregular progress to which the author was committed, but there can be no reservations as to its necessity to the development of Rolland's ideas on the role

78. Ibid.

of music in society. The author sets out, momentarily leaving his hero in stasis, to attack the empty, imitative, and pretentious artistic life of the self-proclaimed capital of the cultural world. As his examination proceeds, one becomes aware that the central issue at question is the absence of a genuine public on which to construct a musical tradition.

La Foire sur la Place is the first indication of one of the real reasons behind Rolland's choice of a German rather than a French musical hero: [79] his novel is in great part a polemical dialogue with the neighboring state. There are very few criticisms of Parisian musical life in *La Foire sur la Place* which are not contained in Rolland's study "Paris als Musikstadt" in *Die Musik*.[80] But Rolland's use of the first impressions of an outsider, an exiled German of high musical sensibility and honesty, allows him the luxury of destroying the milieu he describes before setting about the task of rebuilding the "house" from its ruins. Within the context of a roman-fleuve, the author can afford to set aside one or two volumes for the purpose of exhausting the complaints which would have defeated the polemic aim of his articles.

It is not within the scope of this study to examine in detail Rolland's criticisms of Parisian musical life in *La Foire sur la Place*. In the volume's two hundred pages, the author succeeds in analyzing in detail criticisms which he had already expressed elsewhere. Through the technique of caricature and sweeping generalization, Rolland presents a sampling of practically every imaginable stratum and category of musical life: composers, performers, publishers, critics, musicologists, pedagogues, amateurs, and musical public. He even manages to attack the comfort and ventilation of Parisian concert halls. The criticism is overwhelming and, in the end, fatiguing: whatever justification one may find for this massive attack on the level of Christophe's overall development is largely outweighed by aesthetic criteria. It is small wonder that *La Foire sur la Place,* which represents perhaps one-tenth of *Jean-Christophe's*

79. See also Rolland's article, "Les Origines germaniques de Jean Christophe," *Le Parthénon* (Nov. 5, 1913), pp. 67–68.

80. *Musiciens d'aujourd'hui*, pp. 207–78.

total length, has played such a disproportionate role in inciting critical reaction. The volume tends to overbalance the others by sheer single-mindedness.

Part of this negative effect must be attributed to the fact that the German hero, bearing within him the weight of all the previous volumes, benefits from far greater moral prestige than any other character in the book. Even Olivier, introduced at the end of *La Foire sur la Place,* is too pale and unsubstantial next to Christophe in spite of his biographical embodiment of the author to restore the volume's equilibrium. Thus Christophe's attacks, which Rolland admits are unjust in the following volume, find no rebuttal here and seem in the end to identify the author's point of view with the German tradition as opposed to the French.

Olivier's entry at the close of this volume, however, announces the new direction to be taken in the succeeding ones. Christophe has arrived in Paris like a "Huron" and in the beginning has been able to see only the gaudy surface of life there. Several events give him his first desire to penetrate beneath it: the generous care of a neighboring domestic servant during an illness, his reading of Michelet's *Jeanne d'Arc,* and his encounter with the friend who is going to lead him into the "house" of France to discover its hidden people.

Antoinette: *Olivier Jeannin and the French Character*

Antoinette, the briefest of the volumes of *Jean-Christophe* (it was subtitled *épisode* in the original edition), recounts the life of Olivier Jeannin, the major character of the novel after its hero, and that of his sister, Antoinette. Apart from defining the personality of Christophe's friend and creating a connection with an incident in Germany where Christophe had briefly met Antoinette, the episode provides the opportunity for Rolland to penetrate the life and character of one of those "âmes d'élite" to whom the *Beethoven* was addressed and whose existence was hinted at in the closing pages of *La Foire sur la Place.*

The account of Oliver's childhood in a provincial city (clearly modeled after Rolland's Clamecy), his transfer to Paris during adolescence, his struggles in the unwholesome moral atmosphere of the capital and the beneficial role played by music is filled with details from the author's own life. Reference to Rolland's memoirs reveals familiar events, descriptions, and sentiments on every page of the volume. Rolland put a great deal of himself into Olivier—more, in a concrete sense, than into Christophe—and the reader can sense in every line of this narration what intimate comprehension the author felt for his character. Olivier represents powerfully the pathos of this "moral elite" to which the author belonged by ties of sympathy and kinship. Olivier's life with Antoinette is marked by the deprivation, solitude, moral intransigency, and lonely pride of Rolland's dispossessed elite. In addition, Olivier's literary talent, which he refuses to compromise with the demands of Parisian taste and which has developed without encouragement from outside, makes him a suitable reflection and counterpart to Christophe's genius and a response to the latter's questions concerning French art.

Olivier, however, is an embodiment of the weakness as well as the admirable qualities of this moral elite. He only partially reflects the character of his author, in spite of biographical similarities, and in that partiality he reveals the transitional nature of the moral elite in Rolland's thought. One aspect of this has already been noted in the movement of Rolland's ideas from *Beethoven* to *Haendel*. Here, in *Jean-Christophe,* one can witness this transition in fictional form as Olivier's relationship with Christophe is traced through *Dans la Maison, Les Amies,* and *Le Buisson ardent.*

Olivier is in many ways an extension of the negative spirit of the preceding volume. Most of his strength and courage is provided for him by his sister, who in the end is a martyr to the corrupt society which imprisons the pair in solitude. If Christophe resembles a Rolland endowed with magnified powers and inflated to heroic stature, Olivier contrarily is the image of the author deprived of his almost fanatical convictions, his capacity for enduring isolation in the name of an ideal. Olivier has the stubbornness of the weak, a fitful rebelliousness which can be fired by circumstances, but lacks the stamina to endure. He tends to be driven into himself by the continued attack of circumstances and events. Christophe himself, during the novels following this one, represents the greatest single catalytic force to the realization of Olivier's potentials. But in the long run, Christophe's influence on him exhausts itself, and Olivier turns to the world he has resisted. The conflict between his innate moral superiority and the influence of the compromising majority is resolved only by his death on the barricades, where Christophe has drawn him against his will.

Olivier is too "feminine" a character to represent Rolland's moral nature. Rather, he is Rolland without his "éclairs," the moral victory which the author won in solitude over the atmosphere of the capital. This feminine quality is seen in the passive role Olivier plays in his relationship with Christophe. Christophe is first attracted to him by his resemblance to his sister, whom the composer met in Germany while she was struggling to finance her brother's studies by working as a governess. She was the innocent victim of a scandal caused by Christophe's invitation to a theatrical performance and died before Christophe first encountered her brother in a salon, but Rolland makes the survival of her spirit in Olivier the basis of the two men's friendship.

Olivier's femininity is seen in the role that music plays in his experience. It is not the source of energy, of courage to continue fighting, that Rolland makes of it in *Le Théâtre du peuple*. For Olivier and his sister, music is a consolation and a refuge, an escape from daily reality: "La musique était leur paradis, dans cette dure vie. Elle prit une place immense. Ils s'en enveloppaient pour oublier le reste du monde" (p. 877). This substitute for reality is also the underminer of moral strength which Tolstoy depicts in *The Kreutzer Sonata* and *What Is Art?*, the enemy of action, which saps the energies and whose tantalizing attraction the Russian author feared. Rolland warns here, as in the introduction to his thesis on opera, of its dangers to the weak:

> La musique est un des grands dissolvants modernes. Sa langueur chaude d'étuve ou d'automne énervant surexcite les sens et tue la volonté. . . . Antoinette se sentait si lasse, et comme dans les

bras d'une mère qui la serrait contre son sein! Elle se blottissait
dans le nid doux et tiède; et elle pleurait tout bas. Olivier lui
serrait la main. Personne ne prenait garde à eux dans l'ombre
de la salle monstrueuse, où ils n'étaient pas les seules âmes meur-
tries, qui se réfugiaient sous l'aile maternelle de la Musique. (pp.
877–78)

Their passive absorption in the depths of the concert halls is
carried into their apartment as well, where Olivier supplies distrac-
tion from the day's frustrations by playing the piano. There the
nature of their musical experience is translated into the repertory
which he plays and the quality of his performance:

Il était très bien doué pour la musique: sa nature féminine,
mieux faite pour aimer que pour agir, épousait les pensées des
musiciens qu'il jouait, se fondait avec elles, rendait leurs moin-
dres nuances avec une fidélité passionnée—autant que le lui
permettaient, du moins, ses bras et son souffle débiles, que brisait
l'effort titanique de *Tristan,* ou des dernières sonates de Beethoven. Aussi se réfugiait-il de préférence en Mozart et en Gluck;
et c'était également la musique qu'elle préférait. (p. 879)

Here again, Olivier represents only one aspect of the author's personality. Rolland, in spite of his predilection for Olivier's kind of music,
was capable of powerful renditions of the works his fictional character avoids, as can be seen in Malwida von Meysenbug's tribute to
his performance of the Beethoven *Diabelli Variations,* and the trans-
criptions of Wagner's music-dramas.[81]

In Olivier, musical sensibility is only a facet of his general hyper-
sensitivity. He is a literary representative of overrefined genius which
Rolland found unsatisfactory as the basis for French art in Debussy.
Whatever Olivier's importance as a character in the novel, he is not
representative of that bedrock of French character which Christophe
is seeking for a national school of music founded on the participation and spirit of the people. Olivier's function is suggested at the
end of *Antoinette,* where the two men, surrounded by the alien
atmosphere of a cultural salon, establish their friendship across

81. See *Printemps Romain,* p. 11.

a crowded room. Olivier at that moment is the intermediary between Christophe and the spirit of Antoinette, the dead sister; he is, in Rolland's words, "le messager inconnu . . . un jeune Hermès" (p. 924), who brings the melancholy greeting of the departed spirit. Although this aspect of their friendship is soon succeeded by a more concrete relationship, Olivier remains primarily a messenger and guide, who brings Christophe into contact with the hidden France in *Dans la Maison.*

Dans la Maison: *The Discovery of a French "People"*

Dans la Maison is a mirror image of the world which Rolland describes in *La Foire sur la Place.* More precisely, *Dans la Maison* is meant to penetrate beneath the distorted and superficial reflection of French musical life which the latter volume presents. Having created an unbalanced portrayal of French culture seen through the eyes of his "Huron," Rolland felt pressure from within, from his sense of justice, and from without, from sympathetic but dismayed correspondents more than unfriendly critics, to provide a compensation. Of course, this appreciation is as surcharged as the preceding critique and therefore does not really establish the just measure it was presumably supposed to. In a logical sense, Rolland's procedure is faulty and does not succeed in realizing the balance which constant correction and compensation within a single volume would have achieved. But Rolland's aims were not so much analytical as polemical; his higher allegiance went to his concept of the novel and its hero rather than to objective, rational balance. Christophe develops according to his pattern of violent alternation, and so must his vision of the world.

From the early pages of *Dans la Maison,* Rolland presents his hero's friendship with Olivier as the "key" to the house of France. This friendship is important in a literal sense, but it is also symbolic of the state of mind necessary for true understanding. As Rolland proposed to write a Renaissance history by embracing and "loving" his protagonists,[82] so Christophe's newfound love for Olivier opens the door to understanding, fulfilling the incomplete friendships which

82. See *Cloître*, pp. 175–76.

have preceded it (Corinne in *La Révolte;* Sidonie in *La Foire*) and counteracting his disappointing first contact with the French. The two friends' first thought is to take an apartment together, thereby initiating the symbolic penetration of French character and life.

For Rolland, the house is not merely a metaphorical representation of the fatherland or of human society. It is first of all an image of the self in one of its primary manifestations: the tension between internal life and the world. Rolland applies it, in *Le Voyage intérieur,* to his own personality—the varied "mansions" of his psychological nature. They coexist by a mutual tolerance which becomes at times conflict and at times communion, but they are seen as forever distinct and forever inseparable. His body itself, with its unequal powers, is the type of this "house." Rolland sees his creative effort as a means of enlarging and multiplying the body in compensation for its limitations: "Je ne puis vivre dans mon corps malade, qui ne tient que par l'âme. Il me faut créer d'autres corps." [83]

The house, then, is the image of the spirit in its isolation and solidarity, unity and multiplicity, contraction and expansion. These conflicting qualities of the house were familiar to Rolland, the apartment dweller, who complains in his correspondence of the constant reminders of others' lives, interrupting him by their noise in the midst of his work; yet he makes persistent use in his novels of the sounds of life and music, passing through walls, as a means to establish contact between isolated kindred spirits. Rolland the recluse, jealous of his privacy and independence, and Rolland the humanitarian, to whom nothing human is alien, are conjoined in the image of the house.

In many ways, the secret France of *Dans la Maison* is not strikingly different from the world described in *La Foire sur la Place.* It is not so much a place different from the object of Christophe's previous scorn, as the same country seen in a changed focus, shifted away from the cosmopolitan circles of Paris and toward the provinces and emigrants from the provinces to Paris. It is also frequently the world described previously but seen with different eyes. In

83. *De Jean-Christophe à Colas Breugnon,* p. 131.

acknowledging the negative bias of the preceding volume, Rolland promised this about-face (pp. 636–37). Now Christophe, transformed by his love for Olivier, will see the truth hidden beneath the surface: "renaître jeune et frais dans le corps de l'ami, goûter avec ses yeux le monde renouvelé" (p. 927). The step backward of the previous volume has provided the springboard from which the hero takes his movement and direction toward the final apotheosis—"Et maintenant que le fleuve s'est longuement amassé, absorbant les pensées de l'une et de l'autre rives, il va reprendre son cours vers la mer,—où nous allons tous" ("Aux Amis de Jean-Christophe," p. 1600). This "course toward the sea" in *Dans la Maison* is primarily a reassessment of the musical milieus Rolland criticized in *La Foire:* not, of course, those whose essential immorality or frivolity opened them up to the most severe censure, but those which Christophe castigated for lack of vitality or lack of solidarity with their contemporaries in need. While these criticisms remain valid in the German artist's mind, his friendship with Olivier gives him new insights into the reasons behind them and into a strength of vision and purpose which he could not previously perceive.

He discovers first of all that he has not come into contact with the real French people. Enumerating the people by whose example he has formed his idea of French character, Christophe gives a list which contains members of every nationality but the French: Jews, Belgians, Luxemburgers, Americans, Russians, Levantines. In Olivier's eyes, this "société de débauche," the cosmopolitan elite so influential in Parisian politics, letters, and art, has nothing to do with the real France. He chides his friend and the majority of foreign observers for neglecting the visible and tangible monuments to the French spirit which are masked by the feverish activity and volubility of the ruling class. He points to historical examples of "heroic action" from the Crusades to the Commune and to the tragic quality of French thought, Pascal's in particular. He indicates to his friend the existence of an oppressed majority, "prisoners in our own land," whose voice in government, literature, and art is drowned out by the noise of Paris. They are not aware of their potential strength and numbers—a classless society which has been neglected in favor of the organized proletariat, the politically influential bourgeoisie, and the vociferous "pseudo-elite" who control the press. Because their membership transcends class boundaries, and because they are indefinable by the usual social or political categories, this "real" elite to which Olivier belongs has been betrayed by those who ought to have its interests at heart, as the interests of the authentic France.

Rolland does not succeed in giving this elite a very clear definition, except in negative terms, because of this special character, but his negative description smacks oddly of chauvinism or even racism (which renders even more illogical the accusations of cosmopolitanism and unpatriotism which were leveled against him later):

> On ne saura jamais tout ce que nous avons souffert, attachés au génie de notre race, gardant en nous comme un dépôt sacré la lumière que nous en avions reçue, la protégeant désespérément contre les souffles ennemis qui s'évertuent à l'éteindre,— seuls, sentant autour de nous l'atmosphère empestée de ces métèques, qui se sont abattus sur notre pensée, comme un essaim de mouches, dont les larves hideuses rongent notre raison et souillent notre coeur. (pp. 947–48)

Christophe's later development transcends this racially oriented search for a pure "peuple français," and this diatribe must be understood in its larger context. But the ideas expressed here are reflected elsewhere in Rolland's writings and represent a permanent, if limited, element of his thought.

When Christophe is able to penetrate below the noisy surface of French literary life, he hears new voices, purer and more profound than those of the past; typically, Rolland represents their activity in musical terms to emphasize the epic scope of his tableau:

> C'était une symphonie de voix pures. Pas une n'avait l'ampleur sonore de ces trompettes de peuples que furent les Corneille et les Hugo; mais combien leur concert était plus profond et plus nuancé! La plus riche musique de l'Europe d'aujourd'hui. (p. 951)

He also finds this pure lyricism of the poets in the musical world. What he considered weakness, apathy, and lack of moral fiber in *La Foire,* he hears again under Olivier's direction and discovers qualities he had not suspected. His ears, attuned to the German tradition, have been unable to discern the subtler stream of vibrant life which permeates the creations of the independent French musicians:

> La musique était un de ces petits fraisiers, dissimulés dans l'herbe. Christophe avait d'abord passé, sans le voir, habitué dans son pays à des buissons de musique, bien autrement touffus . . . avec l'aide d'Olivier, il découvrait au milieu des ronces et des feuilles mortes, qui usurpaient le nom de musique, l'art raffiné et ingénu d'une poignée de musiciens. (p. 953)

Beneath the "apparent dilettantism" of this "French chamber music" (the term is opposed to the full-blooded outdoor music of Germany), there is a boldness, a daring which goes far beyond that of his own country—an attempt to renew French art at the sources:

> Il commençait à entrevoir la fièvre de renouvellement, l'inquié- tude,—inconnue de l'autre côté du Rhin,—avec laquelle les musiciens français cherchaient dans les terrains incultes de leur art les germes qui pouvaient féconder l'avenir. (p. 953)

This spirit of research and discovery transcends barriers of time and country, finding the distant roots of French art in ancient Greece, in the "rêves immenses" of the Far East, and in the modes and popular rhythms of the Middle Ages. The French composers were above all struggling to penetrate the laws of the world of sound, the very medium of music.

Christophe finds a spirit which has struggled and come close to defeating the pessimism and emptiness of French art after the debacle of 1870 and the neglect into which music had fallen upon Berlioz' failure to establish a national school. Beyond creating an active workshop of musical art, the generations after the defeat by Prussia had forged something closer to the aim of his search: "un peuple musicien" (p. 954), a foundation upon which the future might carry out the investigations of the innovators, a sounding board against which their works might be tested and proved.

No part of this musical renewal has been more important, Olivier tells Christophe, than the revival of religious faith—Protestant, Jewish, and especially Catholic. Whereas Christophe saw, in *La Foire sur la Place,* an intolerant church spirit inspiring the *Schola cantorum,* he now sees a liberal faith emanating from the provinces, imbued with the spirit of Pascal, whose chief prophet in music is César Franck. In Franck, Christophe sees a "musical saint," whose personal idiosyncrasies, noted ironically in Rolland's diary, do not enter into his portrait in this volume. Rather than an isolated precursor of the *Schola's* decadence, Franck is represented here as the forerunner of a moral and artistic victory: his Belgian origins are disregarded in this tribute to his restoration of the pure French spirit in music—in spite of Olivier's reservations concerning Belgians and other "métèques." The heat of polemics gives rise to many such contradictions.

Christophe then turns his attention from the rather vague panorama which Olivier spreads before him and looks more directly at the "maison" in which he lives and the isolated persons who live there. He discovers the existence in Paris, unconnected with the musical "Fair," of such disparate types as M. Watelet, a former Communard, who carries on impassioned research for a new musical notation to help the spread of musical education; the Arnauds, intelligent and cultivated schoolteachers, for whose timidity and social isolation music is a consolation and refuge; and Commandant Chabran, who passes his reluctant retirement practicing the flute.

These people, in spite of their common residence, are isolated, unable or unwilling to penetrate each other's way of thinking and belief, to realize the unity of French spirit which underlies their apparent differences. Rolland indicates here the role which music can play: it is through Christophe's playing, passing through the walls and echoing through the house, that these separate entities make contact, discover their bonds, and begin to transcend the religious, social, or political quarrels that divide them. Thus the music of the future, realizing its moral and patriotic duty, is to provide the matrix of cohesion for the disparate, unrecognized elements of the nation's people.

There is, once again, a contradiction here. Christophe's music is the creation of German genius, even if an emancipated one. He has not espoused the racial heritage of his hosts; he is essentially a detached, if sympathetic, observer. His music remains his own. How, then, can this product of a foreign culture act toward the unification of a French house in its national spirit? The question remains unanswered in the present volume's search for a nation and a people. Christophe, with Rolland, is committed to a higher cause in the midst of his involvement in the patriotic question. The national bias of the Parisian episodes in the novel is only a facet of more universal, humanitarian aims. The realization of a people is necessary to an eventual transcending of national barriers. The ultimate music is an international code, a direct language open to all "men of goodwill." The immediate need, however, is for utilization of all that is inherent and neglected in the national heritage. Internationalism, in Rolland's vocabulary, is thus distinguished from cosmopolitanism, because it must take its roots in national consciousness to be genuine. Even if, as Olivier says, the real frontiers in art are less those between nations than those between classes, the most urgent need is for the French to find their roots in native soil before there can be any international radiation of what the French, in particular and alone, can give to humanity.

Thus Christophe's music, in spite of its beneficial effects in the "maison," is only a catalyst. What the *immeuble* and the "house" of France need is musical form more germane to its racial and historical spirit. Both of these aspects of French spirit are important, particularly the latter. As Rolland states in a letter to Sofia Bertolini, France is more of an army than a people, linked by the bonds of history rather than the bonds of blood.[84] He renews this idea in *Dans la Maison* a year later: "Ils sont tant de peuples différents, qui travaillent depuis des siècles, côte à côte, sur cette brave terre, que c'est elle qui les unit, c'est elle leur grand amour" (p. 961).

84. *Chère Sofia, 1*, 305 (June 1907).

Christophe attempts, therefore, to prescribe what is needed for the growth of an authentic French musical school reflecting these unities. His prescriptions, for the most part elaborations of the recommendations Rolland made for Paul Landormy's survey in 1904, involve form, subject matter, and style. He recommends utilization of the gifts which have made France preeminent in the Western world—elegance and social poise: "Vous êtes le peuple de l'élégance, de la poésie mondaine, de la beauté dans les gestes, les pas, les attitudes, la mode, les costumes" (p. 1025). These should be employed in the creation of national art forms—splendid ballets and a school of poetic dance. The gift of laughter and comedy should be exploited by serious musicians, who have abandoned the *opéra-comique* as a genre to "musical underlings, grocers of music." The psychological acuity which has made France "a race of novelists" has failed to create "novels in music." The term is imprecise, but Rolland suggests what he means when he says that the popular *feuilletons* of Gustave Charpentier (*Louise,* for example, which in 1900 he accused of banality in reaction to Strauss' praise [85]) do not satisfy his definition of what is worthwhile in the French novel.

For subject matter, Christophe suggests what Rolland did in his articles and letters: rather than what the Germans consider typically French—the frivolous and superficial—he proposes Rabelais as a basis for *opéras-comiques,* "comic epics" instead of comedy of the boulevard. Christophe and Olivier collaborate in "a Rabelaisian epic," *Gargantua,* employing immense forces: symphonic tableaux, soloists and choruses, "des madrigaux à la Jannequin," popular songs, dances, kermis crowds, storms; the model, greatly expanded, would seem to be Berlioz' Romeo and Juliette symphony (p. 1072). For the "novels in music" to replace Charpentier, Christophe calls for "Stendhal for string quartet" (p. 1025).

The ideal material, however, which has been unjustly neglected, is the theme he sees as France's greatest contribution to European civilization—the example of a great democracy at work: "Ah! si

85. *Richard Strauss et Romain Rolland,* p. 134. For Rolland, La Bruyère was the exemplar of French psychological penetration.

j'étais Français, je mettrais en musique votre Révolution: le 14 juillet, le 10 août, Valmy, la Fédération, je mettrais le peuple en musique!" (p. 1025). These were the themes that Rolland treated in his dramatic cycle, *Le Théâtre de la Révolution,* ten years before. In Christophe's imagination, they are on an epic scale calculated to instill courage and national pride in huge popular audiences; this is accomplished by means of the devices which Rolland had found sketched out by Grétry:

> Je veux des symphonies, des choeurs, des danses. Pas de discours! J'en suis las. Silence aux mots: Brosser à larges traits, en de vastes symphonies avec choeurs, d'immenses paysages, des épopées Homériques et Bibliques, le feu, la terre et l'eau et le ciel lumineux, la fièvre qui gonfle les coeurs, la poussée des instincts, des destins d'une race, le triomphe du Rythme, empereur du monde, qui asservit les millions d'hommes et qui lance leurs armées à la mort. (p. 1026)

Christophe recommends a moral reorientation of French music. The racial authenticity of Debussy's music lies not in its peculiar haft-tints and shadows, this "art crépusculaire," but in its fidelity to the French language, its harmonic and melodic freedom, its lightness of orchestration and freedom from Wagnerian rhetoric. The moral atmosphere which Christophe recommends is no less French than *Pelléas et Mélisande.* Rolland's authentic French refuses to be defined solely by "the genius of good taste": he cites Rabelais and the Revolution as evidence to the contrary. Nor does he urge adoption of the "drunken excesses" which pass for vital energy in Strauss' *Salomé.* The two extremes, the geniuses of good and bad taste, are termed manifestations of individual moral decadence in the two countries.

What the French people need is life, energy, and hope for accomplishment of national destiny. The only special requirement is that this energy be grounded in the soil, blood, and history of France, that it reflect the language in which the people think and the setting in which their lives are carried on. Christophe cannot accomplish such a task because his participation in France has been from the outside. If he were French, however, he states what he would do with the materials available to him:

> Je vous mettrais ensemble dans une symphonie chorale *Aux armes, citoyens!*, l'*Internationale, Vive Henry IV!*, *Dieu protège la France!*—toutes les herbes de la Saint-Jean . . . je vous ferais une de ces bouillabaisses, à vous emporter la bouche! Ça serait rudement mauvais,—(pas plus mauvais en tout cas, que ce qu'ils font);—mais je vous réponds que ça vous flanquerait le feu au ventre, et qu'il faudrait bien que vous marchiez! (p. 1053)

"Rudement mauvais" is what it would be: the recipe for bouillabaisse is redolent of Beethoven's for his unfortunate *Battle Symphony*. But the moral bias is clear. Rolland's vision is of nationalistic music, based on the political and cultural heritage of the French, which would be a call to action, a source of energy. Its ultimate aim (as hinted at by the inclusion of the *Internationale*) would be to traverse and erase boundaries between states in the unification of all people. That music constructed according to such precepts would not correspond to the highest aesthetic ideals is, for the moment at least, of little importance. The immediate concern is to find a musical language in which to arouse the people, not to create enduring monuments of art. For the moment, Rolland agrees with Tolstoy's *What Is Art?*, which argues against the "eternal" nature of great art.

Les Amies: *The Creator and His Public*

Les Amies, the first volume of the section entitled *La Fin du Voyage* in the original edition, marks a return to the larger orientation of the work. Once again, the heroic figure of Jean-Christophe becomes the focus, rather than the world surrounding him. Once again the reader is immersed in the stream of the artist's development in his progress toward "the sea." Here there is a parallel stream: Olivier is also near the center of this examination of the creative mind's development, but his progression is toward destruction by the world and his weaknesses.

The "amies" of the title represent two opposing possibilities in the relationship between creative artist and woman. Olivier's marriage to Jacqueline recalls Rolland's disappointing experience with his first wife. On the other hand, Christophe's liaison with the actress Françoise Oudon is characterized by free and constructive interaction between two strong artistic personalities. From Françoise, Christophe draws an understanding of the bond which exists between the artist and his public and which is founded on the internal character of the act of creation, on the relationship between the artist and nature (in its largest sense), and on the function of "real" art in the lives of the people. While not representing a final realization of Christophe's nature as an artist—since by the law of Becoming nothing before death can mark a conclusion in his development—this revelation forms a necessary link in the chain, and the actress has an important role to play in providing the direction of Christophe's first significant creative élan since his arrival in Paris.

In its redefinition of the artist's contacts with nature and the public, this volume gives more evidence of direct Tolstoyan influence than any of those following Christophe's exile from Germany. It still reflects the bias which characterized *La Foire,* where Tolstoy's attack against the artistic elite was put into more concrete terms. One of the most important themes of *Les Amies* is the destruction of Olivier's artistic personality as a result of his acceptance of the society he had previously scorned, under the influence of a socially minded wife. His dissolution is the fulfillment of Christophe's warning that acceptance of the elite is inimical to the free creative spirit, that wealth corrupts the artist and separates him from the earth, the source of his inspiration. In Christophe's dictum, "L'artiste est la voix de la terre. Un riche ne peut pas être un grand artiste," there are reverberations of Tolstoy's letter to Rolland in 1887 (p. 1124). Olivier's gradual absorption in his art for its own sake and his retirement into a private world of literature and self-centered love are the demonstration of this inevitable law. He reaps the fruit of his disregard for essential values in his unhappiness and boredom. Rolland comments on this decline in a paragraph which might be from the text of Tolstoy's letter or from *What Is Art?:*

L'art qui n'a pas pour contrepoids un métier, pour support une forte vie pratique, l'art qui ne sent point dans sa chair l'aiguillon de la tâche journalière, l'art qui n'a point besoin de gagner son pain, perd le meilleur de sa force et de sa réalité. Il est la fleur du luxe. Il n'est plus—(ce qu'il est chez les plus grands des artistes),—le fruit sacré de la peine humaine. (pp. 1150–51)

Like Rolland, Christophe, in search of moral support in his struggle, writes to Tolsoy. He sends him some *lieder,* along with a project for setting one of Tolstoy's stories to music. Unlike Rolland, however, Christophe receives no reply: Tolstoy is unable to comprehend his efforts. Christophe's conclusion is in keeping with the doctrine of his master: Tolstoy shows no interest in his disciples because "great men do not need us" (p. 1179); it is toward the people that artists must turn for their purpose and their satisfaction.

It is in this positive side of Christophe's experience that Tolstoy's ideal of art is most developed in *Les Amies*. Françoise Oudon gives to Christophe a new comprehension of the link between creative artist and audience and the real possibilities, not to say necessity, of communication between them. She reveals the theater to him: not the corrupt one which Rolland castigates in *La Foire,* but the theater which he had dreamed of in the 1890s:

Elle le fit pénétrer dans l'esprit de cet art admirable, le plus parfait des arts, le plus sobre, le plus plein. Elle lui révéla cet instrument magique du rêve humain . . . . Le théâtre, comme la fresque, c'est l'art à sa juste place,—l'art vivant. (p. 1174; Rolland's model for Françoise Oudon is Duse.)

Françoise is not musical, but she is capable of sensing genius and meaning behind "this mysterious language she did not understand." Similarly, while the example of communication between artist and audience which she exposes is dramatic, the underlying experience which her art communcates is equally relevant to Christophe's musical creation. The arts in their individuality are vehicles for something more essential, something they have in common. The actress' mastery reveals psychological truths to Christophe in his search for an enlightened and worthy musical public.

This revelation has to do with the mystical bond which unites artist and public. Rolland makes no attempt to analyze the nature of this bond, which he sees as sporadic, unpredictable, and inspirational. The actress herself knows only that the sole moments which she can really call "acting" in the highest sense come when she transcends the techniques of her art and is transformed into an oracular voice. These moments result not only from her individual talent, but from the collaboration of the faceless multitude seated before her:

> Si réaliste que fût Françoise, et dénuée d'illusions, elle percevait ce pouvoir de suggestion réciproque, ces ondes de sympathie qui relient l'acteur à la foule, ce silence puissant des milliers d'âmes d'où jaillit la voix de l'interprète unique. (p. 1174)

The experience is vaticinal, but not in the way a sybil speaks from a trance which puts her into communion with forces outside of this world. Rather, it is a fleeting intuition of the internal reality of massed humanity, "l'éclair, qui, l'espace d'une seconde, illumine le gouffre, l'âme commune aux millions d'êtres dont la force s'exprime en un seul" (p. 1175).

This revelation gives Christophe a new conception of the composer's relation to his art and public. From the heroic individualism of his years in Germany, the ideal of the artist who first of all is true to himself and only secondarily communicates his experience, he transforms his music into an objective, collective vision: an ideal in which the artist attempts to rid himself of his individuality, to penetrate reality through the community of souls:

> C'était cette âme commune, que devait incarner le grand artiste. Son idéal était le vivant objectivisme de l'aède qui se dépouille de soi, pour vêtir les passions collectives qui soufflent sur le monde. (p. 1175).

Christophe's adoption of this ideal of the objective bard is also a repudiation of nineteenth-century music, whose "disorderly flowering of individual lyricism" is seen as morbid and destructive. His condemnation of "modern music, which talks so much of itself, and mingles its indiscreet confession into everything" is illustrated by an analysis of consecutive settings of Goethe's lyrics, from the first *lieder* set by Zelter (whom Rolland previously criticized for lack of imagination) to those of Hugo Wolf (whose originality Rolland praised in *Musiciens d'aujourd'hui*). The progression is seen as a degeneration: Zelter's settings are "sober and precise," Schubert deforms the lyrics with his "romantic sentimentality," Schumann gives them his "girlish languors," and finally, with Wolf, "le mouvement s'accentue vers une déclamation appuyée, des analyses indécentes, une prétention de ne plus laisser un seul recoin de son âme sans lumière" (p. 1175). Christophe arrives at this judgment reluctantly, since it condemns all of his past creations; but he acknowledges his contamination by this vice and attempts to rid himself of its hold on his creative instincts in order to consecrate his talents to the new vision. In the first part of this study, we saw how this new aesthetic was paralleled by Rolland's research in the life and works of Handel and his publication of what was intended as the first in a series of monographs on him in 1910. Christophe's music in this phase of his development is inspired almost exclusively by the model of Handel and the theories of Tolstoy.

When it comes to putting into practice his new concept of the musician's role, Christophe seeks a musical form in which words and music perform equal functions. Music alone seems insufficient for the message which it must carry to the people. The difficulity lies in finding a text, for the failing of contemporary music is equally true of the other arts. "L'Europe d'aujourd'hui n'avait plus un livre commun: pas un poème, pas une prière, pas un acte de foi qui fût le bien de tous" (p. 1176). Interestingly, the literary vehicles which he ultimately finds adhere to the two categories of art which Tolstoy proposed as "the Christian art of our times."

The first of Tolstoy's categories resembles the usual definition of religious art: "art transmitting feelings flowing from a religious perception of man's position in the world in relation to God and to his neighbor." [86] Denied a proper book from the present, Christophe looks to works of the past for "great simple and humane subjects, speaking to the best in every man's heart" (p. 1177). His search

86. *What Is Art?*, p. 145.

brings him inevitably to the Bible, to the story of Joseph. It is no coincidence that this was also one of Tolstoy's predilections: in Rolland's description of the manner in which Christophe sets the text, the name of the Russian author is cited:

> Il mit ainsi en musique des pages de la Bible, presque littérale-ment transcrites,—la scène immortelle où Joseph se fait reconnaître par ses frères, et, après tant d'épreuves, n'en pouvant plus d'émotion et de tendresse, murmure tout bas ces mots qui ont arraché des larmes au vieux Tolstoy:
>
> "Je ne peux plus . . . . Ecoutez, je suis Joseph: mon père vit-il encore?" (p. 1178).

Tolstoy's other category of Christian art is not normally associated with religion, except in the broad sense which he gives the term. It is "art transmitting the simplest feelings of common life, but such, always, as are accessible to all men in the whole world." [87] Although Tolstoy saw his first category as unsuitable for purely musical expression, he felt this one to be the proper domain of the musician's art. The second of Christophe's popular projects is based on this principle. By coincidence or design, Rolland has him create a purely musical work without literary text. Christophe plans a series of symphonies, "inspired by everyday life." Rolland gives the outline of one of them, a *Sinfonia Domestica* not patterned after Richard Strauss', which Rolland criticized for its bombast and, especially, its literal attempt to depict people, events, and things rather than emotions.[88] Christophe's domestic symphony, unlike this "great contrapuntalist's erudite and childish game," would be based on familial emotions understandable and commonly experienced by normal people—not the "heroic" family of Strauss (p. 1176).

The symphony is Tolstoyan in concept and execution. Tolstoy considered realism an attempt to substitute interest for emotional universality and communication. He used the story of Joseph to illustrate the thesis that the illusion given by detailed description is not necessary to give a sense of truth when the emotions expressed

87. Ibid.
88. *Richard Strauss et Romain Rolland*, p. 144.

in a work of art are genuine and universal. The themes of Christophe's symphony are the sort which Tolstoy would accept as valid: the happiness of a young couple; the death of a child (here Rolland would avoid "any attempt at realistic expression of sorrow"); a strongly rhythmical figure emerging from this sorrow into "a powerful march, full of unconquerable faith"; and finally, a movement representing "the evening of life," in which the earlier themes return transformed, like the emotions they represent, by old age:

> Les thèmes du commencement reparaissaient avec leur confiance touchante et leur tendresse qui ne pouvait vieillir, mais plus mûrs, un peu meurtris, émergeant des ombres de la douleur, couronnés de lumière, et poussant vers le ciel, comme une riche floraison, un hymne de religieux amour à la vie infinie. (p. 1177) [89]

Le Buisson ardent: *The Socialist Crisis*

The second volume of *La Fin du voyage, Le Buisson ardent,* represents an era of crisis and destruction in the life of Jean-Christophe. One might call it a "storm before the calm" leading to the final ascension of the hero's spirit in *La Nouvelle Journée.* The tendencies toward a more socially oriented art followed by Christophe during his Parisian period reach their culmination in this volume: a culmination, at least, in that a limit is reached in this direction. The resolution of his contradictory tendencies in the following volume takes place on another plane, which transcends his previous efforts.

Rolland gives numerous indications in his correspondence of his sense of relief at having unburdened himself of this primarily social phase of his hero's development and his pleasure in taking up again the central movement of his novel. At the end of *Dans la Maison,* he had indicated this in a letter to his German correspondent, Elsa Wolff:

> Je ne puis vous dire combien je suis content d'arriver à la fin de cette série de *Jean-Christophe.* Maintenant je vais pouvoir

89. Rolland's substitution of "infinie" at the end of this passage for "et à Dieu," in the definitive edition, marks the transition of his spiritual ideas.

laisser un peu le monde des idées, et rentrer dans celui des
passions . . . . A chaque volume, à chaque degré que je monte,
j'éprouve le sentiment de l'alpiniste qui gravit une côte: un air
plus léger, une vue plus large, une âme plus sereine.[90]

But there still remained some of the "world of ideas" to be introduced into *Les Amies,* and Rolland only rids his novel of the last
traces of this dialogue between the inner and the outer world in
Le Buisson ardent. Indeed, if one is to believe the preface he wrote
for the definitive edition of *Jean-Christophe* in 1931, his original
plans for the novel included an extra volume to be placed between
Les Amies and *Le Buisson ardent,* in which Christophe was to take
a more active role in the pre-war revolutionary movement (p. xviii).
In the latter volume, however, he manages to close out the social
cycle with éclat, in a symbolic explosion which almost destroys the
psychological balance and the creative powers of his hero. It seems
evident that the violent conflicts which mark the two parts of this
volume were intended to accomplish just such a cataclysmic farewell to the question of socially oriented art, hinting at the revolution
to come, which would decide once and for all such problems.

Although the development of Christophe's art which takes place
in the first part of *Le Buisson* is preceded, like many of the decisive
movements of his life, by a period of stasis or retrogression (the
feeling of peaceful emptiness, the facile exploitation of previous
emotions following his discovery and loss of Grazia), the violent
reaction which succeeds it is a continuation of his previous direction
rather than the start of a new one. The difference between this stage
and the one preceding it is more of degree than of kind: the
musician-hero goes as far as he can along the line of "objective"
popular music and reaches the limit in a destructive spasm which
negates everything which has been accomplished up to that point.
Christophe immerses himself in the cause of the people until the
violence of social forces erupting into the streets of Paris once more
sends him into exile and into a new stage of his creative life.

In his interval of stasis, devoid for the moment of the internal

90. *Fräulein Elsa,* pp. 183–84 (Sept. 1908).

force which habitually occupies him, Christophe is accessible to the murmurs of the proletariat surrounding him. Olivier, after his divorce, leads Christophe into the milieu of radicals and revolutionaries, before his own aristocratic nature, prone more to the love of mankind than to love of men, forces him to retreat in repugnance at the naked hunger, rapacity, and lack of simplicity or idealism of the proletariat in ferment. But Christophe, whose origins and nature give him an understanding of these men, remains and is profoundly stirred.

In spite of his ironic penetration of their motives, Christophe cannot help being moved by this spectacle of turbulence and by the reality of the deprivation it reflects. And in his generosity and naïveté, he cannot help entertaining vague hopes for a renaissance of art from its foundations in the new world promised after the revolution. The revolutionary ferment of the workers appeals to him because of its life, its force and energy. No matter what hopes he might have for the role his music would play as an instrument of moral evolution within the framework of the existing order, capitalism puts the artist in the position of either renouncing success or compromising his art to satisfy the demands of a bourgeois public, whose taste is the heritage of decadence and dilettantism from the past. For all its contradictions and deceptions, the working class is in a healthy state of growth and action. Christophe cannot help responding: "Il était trop vivant pour ne pas être aspiré par l'action la plus vivante qui fût alors" (p. 1276). This world in ferment, this society in the process of Becoming, represents to him a virgin field for the emotions of art, a public uncorrupted by the dead and dying past, eager for spiritual food, "le pain sacré de la musique."

These ideas, which imply a rejection of established order and the doctrinal construction of a new society, are again a passing stage in Christophe's development. They are presented as an intoxication by the new movement (and by the alcohol consumed at its meetings) rather than a systematic approach to the problem of the artist in society. Christophe's demagogic eloquence is a thing of the moment and a source of wonder to him afterward. His partisanship is reflected far more in words than in his musical production, which is limited to "great popular art projects, concerts and theater for the people, which he would have been hard put to define" (p. 1276). Rolland, at the time of the publication of this volume, gave no indication of being committed to the cause which sweeps up his hero: "Pour moi, je vois les vagues passer; mais aucune ne m'emporte. Je suis pourtant, aussi, passionné à ma manière. Mais ma passion m'a hissé sur un îlot, au-dessus de la mer." [91] In the face of threats from right and left his allegiance went to the existing order: "Je sens bien que je suis républicain, toujours." [92]

The entire movement of this penultimate volume of *Jean-Christophe* is one of crisis and dissolution. The central manifestation of this is the adulterous passion which possesses the hero during exile in Switzerland and purges him of the self-assurance which *Les Amies* brought. But Christophe's revolutionary phase is part of this movement, a foretaste of violence and irrationality. It reaches its culmination when Christophe drags Olivier onto the barricades during a May 1st uprising. Olivier loses his life, while Christophe, intoxicated by the violence and aroused to bestiality, kills a man for the first time in his life. His reawakening from the state of animality and his realization of his moral weakness lead to the adulterous affair in Switzerland with Anna Braun and place his involvement with the revolutionary movement in the context of a destructive phase of his development. The entire adventure, seemingly a logical extension of the ideas expressed in *Les Amies,* the emergence from the egotistical self into a more altruistic basis of creation, becomes the first stage of the artist's most profound fall from grace, the most considerable of those downward movements which precede his creative élans. This one is the last:

> C'est la plus terrible crise par où il ait jamais passé; j'aurais voulu l'éviter; mais il me fallait montrer les abîmes qui s'ouvrent dans la vie la plus assurée, aux moments où l'on se croit le plus à l'abri et le mieux défendu. Le livre est plus fait pour troubler que pour soutenir.[93]

91. *Chère Sofia*, 2, 125 (letter of Oct. 1911).
92. Ibid., p. 112.
93. *Chère Sofia*, 2, 122.

Le Buisson ardent thus closes out the humanitarian creative cycle of *Jean-Christophe* with the proverbial bang. Symbolically, this extensive section of the novel which has been dominated by the penetration and expansion of Rolland's house image ends with its destruction. The development of the image pattern implies two necessary conclusions relative to the tension between self and the world in the artist. First, the logical outcome of the violent pressures forcing men into revolution would be a destruction of the artistic tradition which Western civilization has created, and all those who identified themselves with the older forms would necessarily be swept aside (unlike the "two-hatted" Grétry). Second, in terms of the metaphysical implications of Christophe's (or any great artist's) Becoming, these social questions are of secondary importance, an accident or modality of external existence which must give way in the pattern of transcendence to more universal and eternal things: the soul's relationship to all-being:

> L'art le plus haut, le seul digne de ce nom, est au-dessus des lois d'un jour: il est une comète lancée dans l'infini. Que cette force soit utile ou qu'elle semble inutile, même dangereuse, dans l'ordre pratique, elle est la force, elle est le feu; elle est l'éclair jailli du ciel: par là, elle est sacrée, par là, elle est bienfaisante. Ses bienfaits peuvent être, par fortune, même de l'ordre pratique; mais ses vrais, ses divins bienfaits sont, comme la foi, de l'ordre surnaturel. (p. 1424)

IV. CONCLUSION: JEAN-CHRISTOPHE AS A "MUSICAL" NOVEL

In this study, we have examined Romain Rolland's conception of the nature and function of music as embodied in his writings before the First World War, and particularly in his novel, *Jean-Christophe*. We have seen how certain dominant images or patterns—the river, the mountain road, the house—deriving from the principal influences on his aesthetic thought, not only reflect metaphorically the three major characteristics of his idea of music but also represent in themselves, symbolically, the basic patterns of his thinking, his idea of the life of the musician and of the creative personality in general. The interaction and conflict of these image patterns, representing the metaphysical, psychological, and ethical functions of music, are Rolland's most essential conception of the creative life and the pattern of alternation and transcendence which gives his novel its shape and definition. These metaphors played a crucial role in molding Rolland's thought, since his mind tended to crystallize ideas in accordance with formulas or images more than by systematic or analytic processes; they correspond directly to diverse aspects or functions of music, which they express symbolically; and they give shape to the life-stream of the musical artist not only by their direct correspondence with his nature and function, but also, even more strongly, by their conflict, dissonance, alternation, and ultimate resolution. Jean-Christophe is the personification of Rolland's idea of musical creativity, not only because he incorporates these three principles of musical nature, but because his life is constructed, in its Becoming, upon their conflict and resolution.

It is only after examining the nature and relationship of these forces or laws in their essence and effect that one can undertake to define with any satisfaction the nature of *Jean-Christophe* as a "musical" novel. Aside from its place as perhaps the most significant novel of the musician, it has since its creation been referred to as something intrinsically musical, a novel which somehow embodies principles or characteristics normally associated with the art of music rather than the art of literature. *Jean-Christophe* is an attempt to synthesize the personality of the musical creator, as well as the idea and the creation of music. In its conception and structure, it attempts to create a literary form intimately related to the aesthetics and architecture of music. Thus any attempt to characterize the work as a musical novel must center about Rolland's approach to re-focusing the definition of the novel in musical terms. Although much has been written to this date concerning Rolland as a musical writer, there seems to be a good deal of confusion as to what the term really signifies—if anything. Rolland himself contributed to this state of affairs.

The fault common to most attempts at defining the musicality of Rolland's art is the one which Goethe attributed to his appreciators: that of thinking him "in Weimar" when he was already elsewhere. Rolland's pleasure in that particular formula, which he cites in his article on Goethe in *Compagnons de route,* is symptomatic of his need to remain indefinable by any one formula and, by extension, of the essential role played in every aspect of his artistic personality by the conflict of opposing forces. Although this is nowhere truer than in his conception of music, the critics who have undertaken to describe the musical quality of his novel have tended to define music, or Rolland's idea of music, by one or the other of the elements of this dialectic, not by their equilibrium, conflict, and reso-lution. Quotations from a few of them will indicate the divergency of their viewpoints and the partiality of their understanding of Rol-land.

The musicologist Leo Schrade, despite his reservations concerning the political development of Rolland's thought, speaks of *Jean-Christophe* and *Beethoven* in generally flattering terms. But his attempts to characterize the musicality of Rolland's style remain vague: "Musical language seems with Rolland an inborn medium. It appears that he drew poetical inspiration, now from the rhythm of music, now from contemplating music; throughout his life he paid tribute to this art."[1] Rolland's writing is imbued, as Schrade

1. *Beethoven in France,* p. 152.

states, with his musical culture. One is constantly aware, while reading his novel, of the echo of those great musical works in which
his life was steeped and which must have been reverberating in
his mind as he wrote. Their names appear repeatedly in the text
to inform the reader of their renewed presence. Frequently Rolland
inserts musical themes into his text in the form of epigraphs or illustrations: Schubert's *An die Musik,* Bach's *Bleib bei uns, Seid
umschlungen, Millionen* from the finale of Beethoven's *Ninth,* and
so on. In a larger sense, these echoes are reflected in the changing
estimation he gives to musicians of the past. As Jean-Christophe undergoes his numerous modifications of viewpoint, the "background
music" changes accordingly; one can almost hear it. There is nothing
intrinsically musical about these references or echoes, however, any
more than mention of graphic illustrations would prove a "painterly"
manner of literary construction or style. They tell something about
Rolland the man, but far less about his way of writing.

A statement by J.-B. Barrère, on the other hand, shows an attempt
to assimilate musical and literary experience on other, more essential
grounds: "C'est un poète qui a fait de la musique avec des images." [2]
The implication here is that both music and literature in Rolland's
sensibility were functions of a more central quality, imagery, in
which they found their common ground. It is true that in attempting
to express musical creations in terms of a literary form (cf. young
Buddenbrook's improvisations on the harmonium), to translate the
musical experience of his hero into words, Rolland resorts to de-
scriptive passages which evoke images present either in the mind
of the composer as he creates or in the mind of a sensitive listener.
In that sense, Rolland's writing consists of images which lie mid-
way between music and literature and in which the two arts might
be assimilated. It is also true, as was seen in several passages of
Rolland's work, that he felt music emanating from nature as he ob-
served it, completing the process of vision. Conversely, he enter-
tained visions of nature, plastic images, while absorbed in the audi-
tory experience of the concert hall or in the reading of a musical
score (for Rolland had the true musician's ability to appreciate

2. "Romain Rolland, les 'racines' et le 'souffle,' " p. 669.

music on the printed page). His effort to evoke the experience of Christophe's music during the course of the novel is evidence of his belief that this interplay of the arts, which he and many others felt, might be utilized to recreate musical works in literature.

This attempt to describe music in word pictures is the least satisfactory and, I believe, the least important aspect of *Jean-Christophe*'s musicality. Rolland himself, criticizing Strauss' *Sinfonia Domestica,* hinted at the futility of this procedure in the inverse sense, when he blamed the composer for tying his music too closely to a program.[3] He felt that the two "languages" were too dissimilar for such cooperation: the program tended to limit the freedom of the music, and the music did not seem to substantiate the logic and the explicitness of the words used to describe it. In an article for the edition of *Europe* honoring Rolland's sixtieth birthday, Alain, likening the author's descriptions of music to Proust's, characterized both attempts as invalid. This is especially true of nonexistent music as opposed to descriptions of familiar works:

> Il est presque impossible de décrire la musique. Qu'on la commente tant qu'on voudra, on ne la fait toujours point paraître; encore plus évidemment s'il s'agit d'une musique qui n'a point été faite et que personne ne connaîtra. Proust, qui s'oppose à Romain Rolland de toutes les manières, a bien tenté de créer, seulement par des mots, la petite phrase de Vinteuil. C'est un beau jeu, mais ce n'est qu'un jeu. . . . Dans notre *Jean-Christophe,* la musique est plus d'une fois décrite, et vainement. Ce que Christophe invente, je ne l'entends jamais.[4]

Even allowing for varying degrees of musical sensibility in the minds of his readers, this criticism of Rolland's attempts to recreate music seems justified. The author describes the sources of his composer's inspiration in nature, or the psychological state which accompanies his creation, or the images evoked in the spirit of his audience, but he does not succeed in evoking *directly* the musical creation which is meant to be the subject of his description.

3. *Richard Strauss et Romain Rolland,* p. 35.
4. Alain, "Sur le *Jean-Christophe* de Romain Rolland," p. 274.

Others have attempted to explain the impression of musicality that the novel gives by claiming that Rolland wrote literature in musical rather than in literary forms—that the construction of the novel is consciously musical. Rather than resort to traditional novelistic techniques, the author used his competence in music criticism to build his work on traditional musical structures. Rolland did frequently use the word "symphonic" to describe the structure of his novel, and the imagination quickly passes from a figurative to a literal use of the term. He lent a certain air of validity to this assumption in asking Louis Gillet, who was editing a volume of selections from his works shortly before the First World War, to emphasize the musical procedures pursued in the construction of the novel:

> Je souhaiterais notamment qu'on mît en lumière (ce qu'on n'a guère fait, jusqu'à présent) la personnalité, non seulement morale, mais artistique, de *Jean-Christophe,*—ce que l'oeuvre peut avoir d'original, au point de vue littéraire,—et notamment, ses procédés symphoniques:—Préludes et Postludes,—thèmes conducteurs,—développements et crescendo symphoniques et rythmiques (comme l'ouragan de foehn et la révélation nocturne, à la fin du *Buisson ardent*), (ou dans l'orage de la création artistique au début de *la Révolte*)—coda—etc. Je me rends compte que ç'a été, en composant ces livres, ma constante forme de pensée.[5]

There are indeed examples of individual musical forms to be found in the text of *Jean-Christophe*—if one accepts Rolland's assimilation of musical and literary terminology. They are, for the most part, "set pieces" which emerge periodically from the current of the work, interrupting its progress momentarily. They form summations, landmarks, in the flow of the hero's development. The passages cited by Rolland in his letter to Gillet are excellent models of this procedure: a kind of self-contained tone poem in which a theme is developed rhythmically and lyrically, giving an intuition through images of the internal nature of the composer's creative

---

5. *Correspondance*, p. 263.

faculties at work.[6] But is is not the *form* of these passages, their external resemblance to corresponding musical structures like the prelude, symphonic crescendo, or coda, which makes them musical in any profound sense. The same techniques exist in strictly literary terms under different names: preface or prologue, dramatic development, conclusion or epilogue. Even if Rolland categorized these formal divisions under musical names, the nature of the procedure is not necessarily nonliterary.

Stefan Zweig, in his biography of Rolland, comes closer to isolating an element which gives his work its musical nature. Zweig sees it as a necessity for breadth of scope, for cyclical development along a winding complex path, rather than along rigorously logical lines. But he misses the point in attributing this tendency to an ethical rather than an aesthetic necessity: "For Rolland, breadth of scope is a moral necessity rather than an artistic [sic]. Since he would be just in his enthusiasm, since in the parliament of his work he would give every idea its spokesman, he is compelled to write many-voiced choruses."[7] Zweig's explanation is perhaps valid for *La Foire sur la Place* and *Dans la Maison,* where Rolland has his hero embrace successively two opposing sides of the same central issue in order to do justice to the case. These two volumes, however, represent by their primarily polemical nature a break in the development of the novel, insofar as it reflects the life-flow of its hero. They are the least musical parts of the novel for this reason and useless as demonstrations of the basic technique employed by the author.

However, breadth of scope is an attribute of the essential musical quality of the novel. A central idea of the roman-fleuve is the attempt to seize being in its duration, to put the author and reader into direct and continuing communion with its ceaseless movement—to embrace the universe in its Becoming instead of cutting across its flow by a process of analytical dissection. Such an aspiration necessitates breadth and a certain apparent lack of incisiveness. This is the quality in Rolland's prose which several critics have chosen

6. See *Jean-Christophe,* pp. 317, 396–99, 1421–25.
7. *Romain Rolland; The Man and His Work* (New York, 1945), p. 68.

to emphasize. A typical example is found in Charles Baudoin's introduction to *Le Seuil*: "Pour qui pense en mouvement, en dynamisme, en musique, comme Bergson et comme Jean-Christophe, les méandres même errants du chemin contiennent plus de vérité qu'une position même solide." [8] This following of every involution of the stream of movement, whatever its relationship to the more logical pattern which is supposed to dictate literary creation, is also referred to by Jean Bonnerot in describing the style and construction of *Jean-Christophe*: "ce style uniforme et sans éclat, ce style journalier qui paraît fuir au courant de la plume sans ratures." [9] Such a conception of the creative process followed by Rolland implies, however, a variety of automatic writing ("sans ratures"), in which the artist delivers himself over to the spell of his intuition, living and transcribing simultaneously the experience of his vision. This implication is given explicit expression in statements like that of Zweig, who suggests that Rolland wrote in a trance, under the spell of his vision: "Like a musical composer, Rolland followed up particular themes as his mood directed, themes which his artistry was to weave harmoniously into the great symphony." [10] Even more symptomatic of this identification of Rolland's prose style with a certain idea of the nature of musical creation is Alain's statement: "Christophe campe ici et là comme un sauvage; nulle part assis ni fixé. Son furieux amour éclaire en passant telle figure et puis telle autre. Elles n'ont point le temps d'être. Ainsi va la musique." [11]

One may, of course, accept such a definition of the process of musical creation. It is an idea that has antecedents in German philosophy, as in the discussion of Dionysian and Apollonian art in Nietzsche's *Birth of Tragedy*. One of Rolland's letters to Sofia Bertolini, dating from the era of *Dans la Maison*, apparently implies it: "Heureux Christophe! Il est musicien, il n'a qu'à s'abandonner à son flot intérieur." [12] The remainder of this passage, however, takes pains to distinguish between music and literature—specifically Rolland's conception of the latter as embodied in Jean-Christophe:

8. Rolland, *Le Seuil*, p. 13.
9. *Romain Rolland; sa vie, son oeuvre*, p. 93.
10. Zweig, p. 164.
11. Alain, p. 275.
12. *Chère Sofia, 1*, 352.

Mais pour contempler l'univers et pour tâcher de le pénétrer par la pensée, pour être écrivain, il faut une autre nature, qui ne s'abandonne jamais, qui n'est jamais inconsciente, qui a toujours les yeux ouverts, même dans la passion.

Yet this, like many other statements in Rolland's writing, is only a partial truth, a truth in passage. Rolland was fascinated by Beethoven's sketchbooks, in which he could follow the mind of the musician as he painstakingly worked out ideas dictated to him by inspiration, transforming the original themes frequently almost beyond recognition. He underlines the essential role of conscious artistry in the works of Handel, Bach, and most great musicians prior to the Romantic movement, and his enduring appreciation of Wagner was based on a conviction that the composer's greatest works, such as *Tristan und Isolde,* were essentially classical in this sense. Thus Rolland's conception of the workings of the musical mind can in no way be limited to the purely intuitional process ascribed to Christophe in the letter above.

Moreover, a more definitive statement of Rolland's, dating from some time after the termination of *Jean-Christophe,* indicates the extent of his identification of his writing with musical creation: "Je suis, de nature, un musicien qui, détourné de son art, s'exprime en littérature." [13] Rolland leaves no doubt, even at this point, when the focus of his attention has been turned from music by four years of war, that he continued to identify his creative process with that of the composer. He points toward a definition of the musical quality of his literary creation, which lies at a deeper, more essential level of his creative personality than questions of ethics or form.

Rolland gives several descriptions of the process of musical creation during the course of the novel. Among the most striking, and the most familiar, are those found in *L'Adolescent, La Révolte,* and *Le Buisson ardent.* The latter two are referred to in Rolland's letter to Gillet and in most of the critical commentary on Rolland's idea of music. But just as Rolland makes it clear that his hero's successive political, social, and philosophical opinions are to be taken as stages

13. Unpublished letter to the German musicologist Ernst Kurth, Sept. 24, 1918; Fonds Romain Rolland.

of his Becoming, so these acts of musical creation, so often contradictory in nature, are necessary stages in the development of the
composer's ultimate definition of the process. In *La Nouvelle
Journée,* the final volume of the novel, Rolland attempts to synthesize these contradictory stages into an all-encompassing view. It is
surprising that little reference has been made to this description, because the author's characterization of his own creative process bears
a striking resemblance to what is presented in the novel metaphorically.

The dominant astronomical metaphor of this passage, placing
Christophe's musical creation in a transcendent, metaphysical context, represents original inspiration as an unformed, chaotic universe before the Creation, filled with latent power: "D'abord, une
torpeur vague et puissante, l'obscure joie de la grappe pleine, de
l'épi gonflé, de la femme enceinte qui couve son fruit mûr" (p.
1565). The first distinguishing quality to enter into the marshaling
of this chaos is rhythmic motion, the inherent energy of latent forces
manifesting itself by its own internal law: "De cette musique
sombre et dorée, comme un rayon de miel d'automne, peu à peu se
détache le rythme qui la mène; la ronde des planètes se dessine; elle
tourne." Up to this point, the inspiration is autonomous. It contains
the substance, the undirected energy, of the finished work. Rhythm
has unleashed a wild and unbridled motion, and it remains for the
will to take control of it, to jump on the back of this "rêve hen-
nisant qui passe" (the metaphor shifts: one is no longer dealing
with unmasterable cosmic forces but with the "domestication" of
force by human capacities). Drawing its grasp of reality from experience, the will, identified here with reason, is the instrument of
this transformation of substance into form. Reason must guide the
will in its efforts to "break" the wild mustang by penetration of the
substance and its natural rhythm: "L'esprit reconnaît les lois du
rythme qui l'entraîne; il dompte les forces déréglées, et leur fixe la
voie et le but où il va. La symphonie de la raison et de l'instinct
s'organise. L'ombre s'éclaire" (p. 1565).

The circular path of intuited rhythmic movement (the planets) is
transmuted into a defined pattern going from its introduction to a

final objective, with landmarks along the way to indicate direction and progress (the route, which also suggests the river image dominating the novel). Nuclei of individual worlds, which reflect the cosmos in which they are contained, develop on their own scale, microcosmically, as the pattern of the larger development takes shape:

> Sur le long ruban de route qui se déroule, se marquent par étapes des foyers lumineux, qui seront à leur tour dans l'oeuvre en création les noyaux de petits mondes planétaires enchaînés à l'enceinte de leur système solaire. (pp. 1565–66)

Then there is light. "A présent son visage surgit de l'aube incertaine." Reason once again yields to the senses in order to give color to the work. "Tout se précise: l'harmonie des couleurs et le trait des figures." In a moment of conscious abnegation of its mastery, the artist's reason allows the untrammeled play of the senses, of all the irrational qualities of the sentient being. "La cassolette de mémoire s'ouvre, et ses parfums s'exhalent. L'esprit déchaîne les sens; il les laisse délirer, et se tait; mais, tapi à l'affût, il guette et il choisit sa proie" (p. 1566).

When the schema of the work has been given flesh and color by the senses, the composer's rational faculties once again take over, endowing the work with its final concordance in the grand design —consistency and spiritual truth. At the end, the metaphor once again is turned, and the shapeless world-in-birth becomes a monument of the spirit, a cathedral representing the marshaling of substance by reason and vision into an edifice whose religious significance points to the source of all creation. A certain confusion between God the Creator and the musician, creator of monuments to the glory of God, appears in the final stage of this process:

> "Et Dieu contemple son oeuvre. Et il voit qu'*elle n'est pas bonne encore.*"
>
> L'oeil du maître embrasse l'ensemble de sa création; sa main parfait l'harmonie.
>
> Le rêve est accompli. *Te Deum.* (p. 1566)

Either the artist *is* God, and his work is a universe which exists in and of itself, sufficient unto itself; or else the artist is an architect of cathedrals which exist for the magnification of a God whose works transcend the monuments of art. For the moment, at least, Rolland leaves this ambiguity unresolved. It remains one of the last transitional stages of the hero's Becoming and of Rolland's definition of the nature of art.

Fittingly enough in this novel whose form is identified with its hero's life-stream, the resolution is reserved for the period immediately preceding the death of Jean-Christophe. Here the apparent confusion between the godlike creator and the creator as prophet of God forms the material for the final resolution of the dissonances composing Christophe's life. Near the end of *La Nouvelle Journée,* the composer is on the brink of renouncing, once again, not only the music which he has created prior to his latest period—one of "Raphaelian" calm inspired by the experience of Italy—but all musical, indeed all artistic creation. Following the natural direction of his lifelong tendencies, after the loss of his last earthly attachments Christophe gradually becomes separated from his life: "Il s'éloignait de son corps. Ce corps malade et grossier . . . . Quelle indignité d'y avoir été enfermé, tant d'années! Il le regardait s'user, et il pensait:—il n'en a plus pour longtemps" (pp. 1586–87).

In this bodily decline, only the eternal quality of his music seems to grant any reason for existence and consoles him for the oblivion which death will bring. Christophe finds justice in the fact that his music will survive his body, for music represents the best of himself, "le plus vrai, le seul vrai de moi-même." The body has been an engine for creation, a dispensable shell which, having fulfilled its purpose, can now be discarded. Yet a reaction to this thought sets in as well. Christophe carries the idea of dispensability one step further: he begins to consider music as another aspect of his terrestrial and therefore ephemeral self:

> Mais, peu de temps après, il sentit qu'il devenait aussi étranger à son oeuvre qu'à lui-même. L'enfantine illusion de croire à la durée de son art! Il avait la vision nette non seulement du peu qu'il avait fait, mais de la destruction qui guette toute la

musique moderne . . . . Nos constructions sonores, où chantent nos passions, seront des temples vides, s'écrouleront dans l'oubli. . . . Et Christophe s'étonnait de contempler ces ruines, et de n'en être pas troublé. (p. 1587)

Christophe's direction is leading him toward a transcendent reality. In the light of this final ascension, art, in the series of superposed world planes, becomes as illusory as the physical life of its creator: "L'art est l'ombre de l'homme, jetée sur la nature. Qu'ils disparaissent ensemble, lampés par le soleil! Ils m'empêchent de le voir" (p. 1587). If the creative artist, in the highest evolution of his nature, becomes equivalent to God the Creator, then the ephemeral, ersatz creative efforts represented by music, painting, or literature become necessarily objects of scorn. They are illusions, shadows of the ultimate and only real creative act, which is nothing less than the Creation. If the artist is divine, then he can only be so in the fullest sense. He must achieve the transcendence of himself and participate in the divinity of the highest creation. Music is a product of the human mind's limitations, its attempts to fathom the unfathomable and reduce to its own terms the Creation. Its supposed metaphysical validity, its representation of the direct intuition of divine being, disappears in confrontation with the ultimate Reality which the hero feels on the verge of knowing. He casts aside the companion of his lifetime, impatient for this ultimate step in his development which will carry him beyond human existence to all-being: "Mais moi, je veux voir ton visage, Jéhovah! Dût-il m'anéantir, je veux entendre le tonnerre de ta voix. Le bruit de l'art me gêne. Que l'esprit se taise! Silence à l'homme!" (p. 1588).

The composer stops short of this renunciation. Suddenly, without transition, Rolland has Christophe recant. The habits of a lifetime are too strong, the role of music has been too much a part of his earthly existence, and he himself is too human to pretend to the revelation of this final transcendence. He finds himself unconsciously noting down music in the midst of his supposed renunciation. Addressing himself to his art, he recommits himself to the human scale, to the limitation of his artistic Becoming by the boundaries of human experience and therefore by art itself:

—O ma vieille compagne, ma musique, tu es meilleure que moi.
Je suis un ingrat, je te congédie. Mais toi, tu ne me quittes
point; tu ne te laisses pas rebuter par mes caprices. Pardon!
tu le sais bien, ce sont des boutades. Je ne t'ai jamais trahie,
tu ne m'as jamais trahi, nous sommes sûrs l'un de l'autre. Nous
partirons ensemble, mon amie. Reste avec moi, jusqu'à la fin!
Bleib bei uns. (p. 1588)

At this point, Rolland inserts a passage of the Bach cantata's score
as an epigraph. In his final definition of the composer as creator,
Rolland is in effect resolving the ambiguity which characterizes his
hero's creative process in the closing stage of his life. For the first
time, the resolution movement is downward. Rolland poses a limit
to the creative mind's capacity for progress toward perfection. No
matter how high the hero may rise, his limits are those of the human
condition. Christophe the artist is a builder of cathedrals, monuments of man's ingenuity, insight, and devotion to God. He is not
to be assimilated with God the Creator. His creations, although
they may partake of divine nature, as does man himself, are not
autonomous universes, existing eternally and rivaling God's creation. Yet man's constructions testify to the divine spark which has
descended on him and to the dignity which he has succeeded in
achieving through centuries of applying his divine gifts—reason and
intuition. Ultimately, this metaphor represents a resolution of the
novel-long struggle between socially oriented and self-sufficient art:
the cathedral is both an aspiration toward the divine, the transcendent, and a monument to man's perfectibility, beckoning humanity
toward its earthly fulfillment.

Rolland's letter to Ernst Kurth in September 1918 contains a
description of his method of literary composition which is strikingly
similar to the idea of musical composition presented above:

Il vous intéressera peut-être de savoir comment la création se
présente, le plus souvent, chez moi. Elle débute, dans le sub-
conscient, par une nébuleuse, non pas immobile, mais vibrante,
tournoyante. (Ou plutôt, je le sens qui, des espaces lointains,

obscurs, silencieux, s'approche en grondant, et fait son irruption aux limites de mon univers conscient). Dès lors, ce qui domine, dans la perception que j'ai d'elle, c'est son potentiel d'énergie, l'élan, la rapidité, la direction, le dessin de la ligne de course, soit montante, d'un seul jet, soit montante et descendante, comme des "montagnes russes."

C'est ainsi que j'ai conçu *Jean-Christophe*. Avant de connaître le contenu de sa vie, les incidents, les personnages, le nombre de ses années, ou des volumes de l'oeuvre,—j'avais en moi l'impulsion du projectile lancé, de la parabole décrite, du tremblement de l'air, et j'étais emporté par elle. Ensuite venait la détermination des points de passage. Et puis, la découverte, progressive, inattendue, du peuple de sentiments et d'êtres qui remplissaient mon petit royaume.—Mais l'essentiel et le point de départ est dans la joie puissante de ces énergies obscures et vibrantes. Leur expression précise est une déperdition partielle. L'art consiste à les capter aussi bien que possible. Mais sans elles, il n'est rien, qu'un mécanisme mort.[14]

The principal elements are there: an initial chaos; the sense of dim, undirected latent energy; the increasing awareness of linearity and direction; the overall conception which precedes the consciousness of detail; the landmarks which gradually take their place along the line of development; and finally the color and form which will complete the work. The relationship between this overall conception and the sense of motion, of rhythm, is important. Rolland from the beginning conceived his novel in terms of a general curve of development, a rising curve—or rather, a rising and falling one, tending upward: in Renan's expression, not a roller coaster, but "une route en lacets qui monte." The shape of Rolland's novel is an architecture based on the interaction of theme, rhythm, conflict, and plastic linearity, in the way that a symphony of Beethoven's is constructed on motif, rhythm, harmony, and development.

It is in this way that *Jean-Christophe* may be seen as a musical novel. Rolland's idea of the workings of his literary art is in close

14. Fonds Romain Rolland.

accord with his definition of musical creation in the closing chapters of the novel. He did not arrive at this definition only by following the meanders of his intuition until the necessary end of the book: it is to be found in his notes and letters and in the initial idea of the musical novel. It also can be found in Rolland's plan for the construction of *Orsino,* the first of his Renaissance dramas:

> Poser dans chacun des premiers actes un thème de passion qui se développe librement. Au dernier acte, opposer entre eux et superposer les thèmes. Construire, avec un robuste contrepoint, complexe et plein, où se mêlent, sans qu'aucun perde sa forte caractéristique, les motifs d'êtres qui composent l'*Etre* total de la symphonie.[15]

It is evident as well in the original statement of his project to write a musical novel, around 1890, long before the character of his hero was defined: "Toutes les parties en seraient issues d'un même thème général et puissant, à la façon d'une symphonie, bâties sur quelques notes exprimant un sentiment, qui se développe en tous les sens, grandit, triomphe ou succombe, au cours de l'oeuvre." [16]

The mechanism of this connection between theme, rhythm, and architecture is clarified in a letter of the same period to Clotilde Bréal, Rolland's fiancée. In this letter, ten years before writing *Beethoven* (which was, ironically, to grow out of their divorce), Rolland developed some of the basis of his ideas on this mechanism:

> Une phrase musicale dans un grand esprit, (comme un détail d'architecture), ne vaut pas seulement par elle-même, mais par son enchaînement avec ce qui précède et ce qui suit. Tout est logique dans une oeuvre de Beeth[oven,] on ne doit pas juger, par le détail d'abord, puis l'ensemble ensuite,—mais d'abord se pénétrer du sentiment d'ensemble et de là descendre au détail pour l'éclairer.[17]

By adapting this conception of architecture to the novel, Rolland hoped to bring fresh life to a decadent genre, the nineteenth-century

15. Cited in "Le Grain de Vie," p. 208.
16. Ibid., p. 203.
17. Unpublished letter, 1892; Fonds Romain Rolland.

roman d'analyse. Renovation of form and literary concept was closely related in his mind to moral renovation, an idea which haunted him throughout his life, particularly during the idealistic period preceding the First World War. The connection can be seen most clearly in a passage from his diary, dated Rome, March 1890:

> L'ancien roman a pour matière les faits, reliés soit par la logique raisonneuse, soit par le hasard des événements.
>
> Le roman musical a pour matière le sentiment,—et de préférence les sentiments les plus généraux, sous leur forme la plus intense, la plus complète. Il ne doit pas les analyser (ce serait de la critique), mais les faire revivre sous le vêtement de telle ou telle apparence, de tel ou tel personnage, en qui ces sentiments s'incarnent et qui en sont la proie. Toute partie du roman musical doit jaillir d'un sentiment général et puissant, fortement éprouvé. Comme une symphonie est bâtie sur quelques notes exprimant une Passion, qui se développe en tous sens, grandit, triomphe, ou succombe, un roman musical doit être la floraison d'un sentiment qui en est l'âme.[18]

Although Rolland was to turn away from the tragic pessimism, the cult of the vanquished hero, which is evident in his works prior to the turn of the century and which can be felt in the above passage, the conception of the novel outlined there remained with him while he was creating *Jean-Christophe.*

If Rolland's novel is musical in its intrinsic nature, it is because he conceived it in the way he felt to be that of the symphonic composer. Like a symphony, the novel was for him an immense structure, paradoxically complex and simple at the same time, built on certain themes, rhythms, and dominant sentiments, dictated from the author's intuition of formless substance, having its own internal laws, and conceived in its architectural whole, its grand lines, from the beginning. It had a shape, a direction, and a final goal which were imagined before anything was put into material form; and it was constantly directed, in the midst of its apparent wanderings, by the overall conception, its internal relationships, and the laws of its

18. Unpublished fragment of Journal; Fonds Romain Rolland.

development—which were neither those of the traditional novel nor those of "la logique raisonneuse." If there are imperfections in the details of its working out, it is not because the novel took shape in haste or from day to day; it is because it was conceived on a monumental scale and was not meant to be "regardé à la loupe." Rolland cites Gluck, answering criticism of his operas:

> Supposez un homme qui pour mieux voir les peintures de la coupole du Val-de-Grâce monte dans la coupole, et, le visage appliqué au mur, crie au peintre qui est en bas: "Eh! Monsieur, est-ce un nez? est-ce un pied? qu'avez-vous prétendu faire?" Le peintre lui répondrait: "Eh, Monsieur, descendez, vous le verrez aussi bien que moi."—Certaines oeuvres sont faites pour être vues de loin, parce qu'il y a en elles un rythme passionné qui mène tout l'ensemble et subordonne les détails à l'effet général. Ainsi Tolstoï, ainsi Beethoven.[19]

Thus Beethoven and Gluck, who are "grandes âmes," composed carelessly—not for lack of ability to do correct work, but because the nature of their vision, the scope of their imagination, demanded such large-scale, coarse-grained technique. Viewed close up, this coarseness seems an untidy jumble. That is why Rolland insisted that "purists" would never be capable of understanding great music. On the other hand, when seen from the viewpoint of the composer or author, from which point the eye can embrace the entire structure, all of the dissonant or confused detail becomes clarified as part of the larger rhythmic or plastic pattern of the work. This is the way the great nineteenth-century symphonic literature must be appreciated: the nature of such music, its architecture, requires that the listener submerge himself in the work's stream of duration, that he exist in unison with it and experience the composer's intuition in the same rhythm in which it dictated itself to him. At the same time, part of the listener's consciousness must remain separate from this submerged intuition, analyzing and organizing the experience which the rest of the mind is undergoing, tracing direction and

19. Letter to Mme Louise Cruppi, June 15, 1911, cited in Alfred Saffrey's preface to *Une Amitié française*, p. 161.

development, relating and balancing rhythms, and synthesizing the apparently unrelated or dissonant antithetical experiences which occur from moment to moment. This emergent segment of consciousness is, in part, the ear of memory. But it is also another ear, a tension toward the future, which relates the end of the work to all the parts as they are immediately experienced. As Alain writes:

> Tout le livre est musique par un mouvement épique qui va selon le cours du temps, et par un genre de souvenir en avant de soi, et aussitôt passé, aussitôt recouvert. Même un lent Adagio n'attend pas; il nous emporte; on sent d'autant mieux l'inflexible loi par ce mouvement majestueux, sans violence ni faiblesse.[20]

This is not the unity of the monolith alone, however; it is the grand harmony of contrasts. Rolland considered the essence of the musical mind to be the power of memory, of foresight, of emergent reason rising above the turmoil of discords, dissonances, false resolutions, modulations, enharmonics, and all the mysteries of detail which make up the musical experience. It is that same power which he felt to be the focus of the act of literary creation in himself, the transcendent force which emerges from the turbulence of internal conflicts, passions, and events and remains clear and omniscient through everything which absorbs the intuition and senses:

> Quand on a une source de vie assez abondante pour qu'elle ne risque pas de se dessécher, à la lumière de la conscience, il y a une ivresse d'âme à se sentir emporté par des forces intérieures, et à voir ces forces qui vous emportent,—à jouir de l'heure qui passe, et à lire pourtant en elle les heures qui viendront. Il est beau de voir clair, toujours.[21]

The heroic life of Jean-Christophe was to take shape as a function and an expression of this power, the attribute of the great symphonists—passing through the contradictory stages of his development, seeming to lose direction and to change in nature from

---

20. 'Sur le *Jean-Christophe* de Romain Rolland," p. 274.
21. *Chère Sofia, 1,* 352.

chapter to chapter, volume to volume, but always returning inevitably to the route which the author had plotted, always embodying the law of development upon which his character was constructed, and always, somehow, retaining the original given substance of his personality through profound changes in environment, age, aesthetic doctrine, and political belief. Rolland's vision of music and of the novel's effect on a world on the brink of its apocalyptic struggle was one in which the inflexible law of Becoming, through its resolution of intermediary stages of dissonance, would eventually bring humanity to the level of exaltation which marks Christophe's final stage: the bright peace above the battle. Like Rolland's Empedocles, Christophe was to sing "son chant d'espoir et de paix, la splendide symphonie de la Vie universelle, dont les dissonances cruelles périodiquement se résolvent en des accords de lumière." [22] If both music and the novel took another direction in the years following the creation of *Jean-Christophe,* it was due to the birth of a new era growing out of the upheaval of the First World War. *Christophe* remains as a summit of the idealistic novel and as the summation of a concept of art which still has its nostalgic attractions today.

22. Romain Rolland, *Empédocle d'Agrigente,* pp. 26–27.

BIBLIOGRAPHY

Works by Romain Rolland

Jean-Christophe, Paris, *Cahiers de la Quinzaine*, 1904–12.
   L'Aube, Ser. 5, No. 9, 2 fév. 1904.
   Le Matin, Ser. 5, No. 10, 16 fév. 1904.
   L'Adolescent, Ser. 6, No. 8, 10 jan. 1905.
   La Révolte:
      Sables mouvants, Ser. 8, No. 4, 13 nov. 1906.
      L'Enlisement, Ser. 8, No. 6, 11 déc. 1906.
      La Délivrance, Ser. 8, No. 9, 2 jan. 1907.
   La Foire sur la Place, Ser. 9, Nos. 13–14, 17–24 mars 1908.
   Antoinette, Ser. 9, No. 15, 31 mars 1908.
   Dans la Maison, Ser. 10, Nos. 9–10, 16–23 fév. 1909.
   Les Amies, Ser. 11, Nos. 7–8, 25 jan.–8 fév. 1910.
   Le Buisson ardent, Ser. 13, Nos. 5–6, 31 oct.–7 nov. 1911.
   La Nouvelle Journée, Ser. 14, Nos. 2–3, 6–20 oct. 1912.

The definitive edition of *Jean-Christophe* was published in Paris by Albin Michel in 1931.

Musicological works

   Les Origines du théâtre lyrique moderne. L'Histoire de l'Opéra en Europe avant Lully et Scarlatti (Bibliothèque des Ecoles françaises d'Athènes et de Rome, 1877–1930, fasc. 71), Paris, E. Thorin, 1895. (Doctoral dissertation, Université de Paris.)
   Beethoven, Vies des hommes illustres, Paris, *Cahiers de la Quinzaine,* Ser. 4, No. 10, 24 jan. 1903.
   Musiciens d'aujourd'hui, Paris, Hachette, 1908.
   Musiciens d'autrefois, Paris, Hachette, 1908.
   Haendel, Paris, Alcan, 1908.
   Voyage musical au pays du passé, Paris, Hachette, 1920.

Beethoven: les grandes époques créatrices, 6 vols. Paris, Editions du Sablier, 1929–45.

Biographies, essays, and miscellaneous collections

Le Théâtre du peuple, Paris, *Cahiers de la Quinzaine,* Ser. 5, No. 4, 24 nov. 1903. An enlarged edition was published in Paris by Hachette in 1913.

La Vie de Michel-Ange, Vies des hommes illustres, Paris, *Cahiers de la Quinzaine,* Ser. 7, No. 18–Ser. 8, No. 2, 26 juin–16 oct. 1906.

Vie de Tolstoï, Vies des hommes illustres, Paris, Hachette, 1911.

Compagnons de route: Essais littéraires, Paris, Albin Michel, 1936. (Contains articles dating from 1900 to 1935, published in the *Revue d'art dramatique, Europe,* and elsewhere.)

Péguy, 2 vols. Paris, Albin Michel, 1945. (Edition in one volume with original paging: Buenos Aires, Viau-Feugere, 1946.)

Correspondence, memoirs, and autobiographical essays

Mémoires, et fragments du journal, Paris, Albin Michel, 1956. ("Souvenirs de jeunesse" and memoirs up to 1900.)

Le Cloître de la rue d'Ulm: Journal de Romain Rolland à l'Ecole Normale (1886–1889), in *Cahiers Romain Rolland, 4,* Paris, Albin Michel, 1952.

Printemps Romain: Choix de lettres de Romain Rolland à sa mère (1889–1890), avec un texte de Malwida von Meysenbug, in *Cahiers Romain Rolland, 6,* Paris, Albin Michel, 1954.

Retour au Palais Farnèse: Choix de lettres de Romain Rolland à sa mère (1890–1891), introduction de Sofia Bertolini Guerrieri-Gonzaga, in *Cahiers Romain Rolland, 8,* Paris, Albin Michel, 1956.

"Le Grain de Vie (extrait des mémoires de Romain Rolland)," *Mercure de France,* 300 (1 juin 1947), 201–13.

Choix de lettres à Malwida von Meysenbug, avant-propos de

Edouard Monod-Herzen, in *Cahiers Romain Rolland, 1,* Paris, Albin Michel, 1948.

Correspondance entre Louis Gillet et Romain Rolland: Choix de lettres, préface de Paul Claudel, in *Cahiers Romain Rolland, 2,* Paris, Albin Michel, 1949.

Une Amitié française: Correspondance entre Charles Péguy et Romain Rolland, présentée par Alfred Saffrey, in *Cahiers Romain Rolland, 7,* Paris, Albin Michel, 1955.

Richard Strauss et Romain Rolland. Correspondance. Fragments de Journal, avant-propos de Gustave Samazeuilh, in *Cahiers Romain Rolland, 3,* Paris, Albin Michel, 1951.

Une Lettre inédite de Tolstoï, introduction de Romain Rolland, Paris, *Cahiers de la Quinzaine,* Ser. 3, No. 9, 24 fév. 1902. (Letter to Romain Rolland of 1887.)

Chère Sofia: Vol. I. Choix de lettres de Romain Rolland à Sofia Bertolini Guerrieri-Gonzaga (1901–1908), préface de Umberto Zanotti-Bianco, in *Cahiers Romain Rolland, 10,* Paris, Albin Michel, 1959.

Chère Sofia: Vol. II. Choix de lettres de Romain Rolland à Sofia Bertolini Guerrieri-Gonzaga (1909–1932), in *Cahiers Romain Rolland, 11,* Paris, Albin Michel, 1960.

Fräulein Elsa; Lettres de Romain Rolland à Elsa Wolff, in *Cahiers Romain Rolland, 14,* Paris, Albin Michel, 1964.

Deux hommes se rencontrent; Correspondance entre Jean-Richard Bloch et Romain Rolland, 1910–1918, in *Cahiers Romain Rolland, 15,* Paris, Albin Michel, 1964.

De Jean-Christophe à Colas Breugnon. Pages de Journal, préface de Jérôme et Jean Tharaud, Paris, Editions du Salon Carré, 1946. (Period of 1912–13.)

Journal des années de guerre (1914–1919): Notes et documents pour servir à l'histoire morale de l'Europe de ce temps, préface de Louis Martin-Chauffier, texte établi par Marie Romain Rolland, Paris, Albin Michel, 1952.

Empédocle d'Agrigente, suivi de l'Eclair de Spinoza, Paris, Editions du Sablier, 1931. (Part of unpublished memoirs.)

Le Voyage intérieur, Paris, Albin Michel, 1942.

Le Seuil, précédé du Royaume du T, Collection Action et Pensée, 21, Geneva, Editions du Mont-Blanc, 1947. (Sequel to *Le Voyage intérieur.*)

Articles on music

"Don Lorenzo Perosi," *Revue de Paris* (15 mars 1899), pp. 443–48. (Later published in *Musiciens d'aujourd'hui.*)

"Richard Strauss," *Revue de Paris* (15 juin 1899), pp. 769–89. (Later published in *Musiciens d'aujourd'hui.*)

"Tristan," *Revue d'art dramatique, 8* (5 nov. 1899), 171–77. (Later published in *Musiciens d'aujourd'hui.*)

"Siegfried," *Revue de Paris* (1 fév. 1902), pp. 188–204. (Later published in *Musiciens d'aujourd'hui.*)

"La Musique et l'histoire générale," *Revue musicale, 2* (juin 1902), 249–59. (Later published as Introduction of *Musiciens d'autrefois.*)

"Vincent d'Indy," *Revue de Paris* (15 jan. 1903), pp. 401–20. (Later published in *Musiciens d'aujourd'hui.*)

"Mozart," *Revue d'art dramatique, 18* (15 jan., 15 fév. 1903), 15–26, 49–57. (Later published in *Musiciens d'aujourd'hui.*)

"Berlioz," *Revue de Paris* (1, 15 mars 1904), pp. 65–88, 331–52. (Later published in *Musiciens d'aujourd'hui.*)

"Réponse à l'enquête de Paul Landormy: l'état actuel de la musique française," *Revue bleue* (2 avr. 1904), pp. 424–25.

"Hugo Wolf," *Revue de Paris, 3* (15 mai 1905), 401–21. (Later published in *Musiciens d'aujourd'hui.*)

"Une fête musicale en Alsace-Lorraine," *Revue de Paris, 4* (1 juillet 1905), 134–52. (Later published in *Musiciens d'aujourd'hui* as "Musique française et musique allemande.")

"Souvenirs sur Richard Strauss," *Les Oeuvres libres,* No. 27, N.S. 253 (1948), 3–18.

Theater

Le Théâtre de la Révolution: Danton. Le Quatorze juillet. Les Loups, Paris, Hachette, 1909.

Les Tragédies de la foi: Saint-Louis. Aërt. Le Triomphe de la raison, Paris, Hachette, 1913.

Studies on Romain Rolland

Biography

Arcos, R., *Romain Rolland,* Paris, Mercure de France, 1950.

Barrère, J.-B., *Romain Rolland par lui-même,* images et textes présentés par J.-B. Barrère, Collection Ecrivains de toujours, 31, Paris, Editions du Seuil, 1955.

Bonnerot, J., *Romain Rolland; sa vie, son oeuvre. Document pour l'histoire de la littérature française,* Paris, Editions du Carnet, 1921.

Di Scanno, T., *Romain Rolland,* Parma, Guanda, 1957.

Doisy, M., *Romain Rolland: 1866–1944,* Brussels, Editions "La Boétie," 1945.

Robichez, J., *Romain Rolland,* Paris, Hatier, 1961.

Seippel, P., *Romain Rolland; l'homme et l'oeuvre,* Paris, Ollendorf, 1913.

Sénéchal, C., *Romain Rolland,* Paris, Editions de la caravelle, 1933.

Zweig, S., *Romain Rolland; sa vie—son oeuvre,* texte français de O. Richez, Paris, Les Editions pittoresques, 1929.

Critical studies and articles

Alain, "Sur le *Jean-Christophe* de Romain Rolland," *Europe, 10* (15 jan. 1926), 272–78.

Barrère, J.-B., "Romain Rolland: les 'racines' et le 'souffle,' " *Mercure de France,* 1092 (1 août 1954), 668–89.

Cheval, R., *Romain Rolland, l'Allemagne et la guerre,* Paris, PUF, 1963.

Fest, O., *Stilistische Untersuchung zu Romain Rolland's "Pierre et Luce". Formentwicklung und Deutung,* Jena, Borna, Noske, 1935.

Krampf, M., *La Conception de la vie héroïque dans l'oeuvre de Romain Rolland,* Paris, Le Cercle du Livre, 1956.

Prunières, H., "Romain Rolland et l'histoire musicale," *Europe, 10* (15 jan. 1926), 300–06.

Roos, J., "Romain Rolland et Spinoza," *Bulletin de l'Association des Amis de Romain Rolland,* No. 42 (déc. 1957), 20–28.

Roy, D. K., *Among the Great,* Bombay, N. M. Tripathi, 1945. (Conversations and correspondence with Romain Rolland and others.)

Schrade, L., *Beethoven in France,* New Haven, Yale University Press, 1942. (Judgments on Rolland's *Beethoven,* pp. 142–75.)

Starr, W. T., *A Critical Bibliography of the Published Writings of Romain Rolland,* Evanston, Ill., Northwestern Unisity Press, 1950.

Miscellaneous Works and Articles

Ansermet, E., and Piguet, J.-C., *Entretiens sur la musique,* Neuchatel, La Baconnière, 1963.

Eckermann, J. P., *Gespräche mit Goethe,* 3 vols. in one, Leipzig, Reclam, 1884.

Goethe, J. W. von, *West-östlicher Divan. Goethes Werke,* Band 6, Weimar, Böhlau, 1888.

Koechlin, C., "Paul Dupin," *La Revue musicale, 4* (1 jan. 1923), 227–41.

Nietzsche, F., *The Birth of Tragedy,* in *The Complete Works of Nietzsche,* trans. W. A. Haussmann, *1,* London, Foulis, 1910.

Peyre Henri, *The Contemporary French Novel,* New York, Oxford University Press, 1955.

Prunières, H., *A New History of Music,* with an introduction by Romain Rolland, trans. E. Lockspeiser, New York, Macmillan, 1943.

Renan, E., *Drames philosophiques,* Paris, Calmann Levy, 1888.

Spinoza, B., *Oeuvres de Spinoza,* traduites par Emile Saisset, 2 vols. Paris, Charpentier, 1878.

Tolstoy, L. N., *The Kreutzer Sonata and Other Stories,* ed. Aylmer Maude, New York, 1924.

Tolstoy, L. N., *What Is Art?,* trans. Aylmer Maude, New York, Scribner's, 1904.

Wagner, R., *Letters of Richard Wagner,* selected and ed. by Wilhelm Altmann, trans. N. M. Bozman, 2 vols. New York, Dutton, 1927.

INDEX